THE TRIUMPH OF
THE RISING

John MacArthur
PUBLISHING GROUP

ESTBLD   MMXXIII

Los Angeles
CALIFORNIA

DESIGNED BY WEKREATIVE CO.
ISBN: 978-1-883973-06-3
PRINTED IN THE UNITED STATES OF AMERICA

THE TRIUMPH OF THE RISING

THE BELIEVER'S VICTORY OVER DEATH

JOHN MACARTHUR

CONTENTS

INTRODUCTION

All Scripture is God-breathed and spiritually profitable for the salvation and sanctification of every believer. Every word of God is pure truth, living and life-giving, powerful and empowering.

For over half a century, I have lived daily with the Scripture in my hands and on my mind—and preached it from the pulpit of the church—and written a series of expository commentaries on each New Testament book, totaling thirty-four volumes.

I am grateful for everyone who is willing to settle in and dig deep in reading a commentary. But only a few take on such an extensive journey, even though every aspect of the Scripture is life transforming. My desire, however, is for many to engage in such a pursuit because they will then experience the benefit and blessing of the deep dive into a biblical book.

I am certain when people have a taste of the riches of Bible exposition they will want more. So I thought we should give them less to develop the hunger for more.

What do I mean by less?

ONE CHAPTER. ONE MONUMENTAL CHAPTER.

So, that led to the development of this series, *The Great Chapters of the Bible*. This series focuses on key portions of Scripture that establish the foundational truths of the Christian faith. The current volume, adapted from *1 Corinthians*, the MacArthur New Testament Commentary, delivers Paul's treatment of the doctrine of resurrection.

I believe that exposition of the great chapters of the Bible will lead many to desire to know the rest of each book and to experience the blessing of knowing the Scripture in its fullness.

01

THE EVIDENCE FOR CHRIST'S RESURRECTION

1 CORINTHIANS 15:1-11

Now I make known to you, brethren, the gospel which I preached to you, which also you received, in which also you stand, by which also you are saved, if you hold fast the word which I preached to you, unless you believed in vain. For I delivered to you as of first importance what I also received, that Christ died for our sins according to the Scriptures, and that He was buried, and that He was raised on the third day according to the Scriptures, and that He appeared to Cephas, then to the twelve. After that He appeared to more than five hundred brethren at one time, most of whom remain until now, but some have fallen asleep; then He appeared to James, then to all the apostles; and last of all, as it were to one untimely born, He appeared to me also. For I am the least of the apostles, who am not fit to be called an apostle, because I persecuted the church of God. But by the grace of God I am what I am, and His grace toward me did not prove vain; but I labored even more than all of them, yet not I, but the grace of God with me. Whether then it was I or they, so we preach and so you believed. (15:1–11)

Unlike most of 1 Corinthians, chapter 15 is devoted entirely to doctrine, and to a single doctrine at that. In these fifty-eight verses, Paul gives the most extensive treatment of the resurrection in all of Scripture.

Just as the heart pumps life-giving blood to every part of the body, so the truth of the resurrection gives life to every other area of gospel truth. The resurrection is the pivot on which all of Christianity turns and without which none of the other truths would much matter. Without the resurrection, Christianity would be so much wishful thinking, taking its place alongside all other human philosophy and religious speculation.

The resurrection was the focal point of every other truth Christ taught. He taught His disciples that "the Son of Man must suffer many things and be rejected by the elders and the chief priests and the scribes, and be killed, and after three days rise again" (Mark 8:31; cf. 9:9, 31). He said, "I am the resurrection and the life; he who believes in Me shall live even if he dies" (John 11:25). The first two sermons preached after Pentecost both focused on the resurrection of Christ (Acts 2:14–36; 3:12–26). Because of that truth, the heartbroken followers of the crucified Rabbi were turned into the courageous witnesses and martyrs who, in a few years, spread the gospel across the Roman empire and beyond. Belief in the resurrection, the truth that this life is only a prelude to the life to come for those who trust in Jesus Christ, could not be obliterated by ridicule, prison, torture, or even death. No fear or dread in this life can quench the hope and joy of an assured life to come.

True New Testament Christianity is a religion of the resurrection. John Locke, the 18th-century British philosopher, said, "Our Saviour's resurrection is truly of great importance in Christianity, so great that His being or not being the Messiah stands or falls with it."

Because it is the cornerstone of the gospel, the resurrection has been the target of Satan's greatest attacks against the church. If the resurrection is eliminated, the life-giving power of the gospel is eliminated, the deity of Christ is eliminated, salvation from sin is eliminated, and eternal life is eliminated. "If we have hoped in Christ in this life only, we are of all men most to be pitied" (1 Cor 15:19). If Christ did not live past the grave, those who trust in Him surely cannot hope to do so.

Without the resurrection, salvation could not have been provided, and without belief in the resurrection, salvation cannot be received. "If you confess with your mouth Jesus as Lord, and believe in your heart that God raised Him from the dead, you shall be saved" (Rom 10:9). It is not possible, therefore, to be a Christian and not believe in the resurrection of Jesus Christ.

The doctrinal problem on which this chapter focuses was not the Corinthians' disbelief in Christ's resurrection but confusion about their own. Paul was not trying to convince them that Christ rose from the dead but that one day they, too, would be raised with Him to eternal life. Nevertheless, to lay the foundation, in the first eleven verses he reviews the evidences for

Jesus' resurrection, a truth he acknowledges they already believed (vv. 1, 11). The five evidences, or testimonies, he presents are: the church; the Scriptures; the eyewitnesses; a special witness, the apostle himself; and the common message.

THE TESTIMONY OF THE CHURCH

Now I make known to you, brethren, the gospel which I preached to you, which also you received, in which also you stand, by which also you are saved, if you hold fast the word which I preached to you, unless you believed in vain. (15:1–2)

The first testimony is not stated explicitly but is implied. The very fact that the Corinthian Christians themselves, and all other Christians everywhere, had received the gospel and believed in Jesus Christ and had been miraculously changed, was in itself a strong evidence of the power of the gospel, which power is in the resurrection of Christ.

By addressing them again as **brethren** (cf. 1:10; 2:1; 3:1; 10:1; etc.), Paul assures those to whom he writes that he recognizes them to be fellow Christians. The term not only expresses his spiritual identity with them but also his love (cf. 15:58).

The apostle tells them that what he is about to say is nothing new to them, but is simply **the gospel which I**

preached to you, which also you received. Not until verses 3–4 does he specify what the heart of the gospel is: "that Christ died for our sins, … and that He was buried, and that He was raised on the third day." The point of the first two verses is that the Corinthian believers were themselves living evidence that this doctrine was true. The fact that they came out of the spiritual blindness and deadness of Judaism or paganism and into the light and life of Christ testified to the power of the gospel, and therefore to the power of the resurrection. It also testified that they already believed in the truth of Christ's resurrection. It was the gospel of the resurrection of Jesus Christ that Paul had **preached** to them, that they had **received,** and in which he assures them they now **stand** and by which they **are saved,** delivered from sin's power and condemnation. Because of the reality of Christ's resurrection and of their trust in it, they were now a part of His church and thereby were evidence of the power of that resurrection.

Paul's qualifying phrase—**if you hold fast the word which I preached to you, unless you believed in vain**—does not teach that true believers are in danger of losing their salvation, but it is a warning against non-saving faith. So a clearer rendering would be, "… if you hold fast what I preached to you, unless your faith is worthless or unless you believed without effect." The Corinthians' holding fast to what Paul had preached (see 11:2) was the result of and an evidence of their genuine salvation, just as their salvation and new life were an evidence of the power of Christ's resurrection. It must be recognized, however, that some lacked the true saving faith, and thus did not continue to obey the Word of God.

Paul's teaching about the security of believers was unambiguous. "For whom He foreknew, He also predestined to become conformed to the image of His Son, that He might be the firstborn among many brethren; and whom He predestined, these He also called; and whom He called, these He also justified; and whom He justified, these He also glorified" (Rom 8:29–30; cf. vv. 35–39; 5:9–10; 9:23; 1 Cor 2:7; etc.). It is only by God's power that we are saved and only by His power that we are kept saved. Our salvation is kept by Christ's holding us fast, not primarily by our holding Him fast. Our holding onto Him is evidence that He is holding onto us.

A professing Christian who holds to orthodox doctrine and living and then fully rejects it proves that his salvation was never real. He is able to let go of the things of God because he is doing the holding. He does not belong to God and therefore God's power cannot keep him. Such a person does not **hold fast the word** because his faith is **in vain.** It was never real. He cannot hold fast because he is not held fast.

Our Lord repeatedly spoke of sham believers who had useless, non-saving faith. The parable of the sower

(Matt 13:1–23) tells us that some of the seeds of the gospel fall on shallow or weedy soil, and that tares often look like wheat, but are not (13:24–30, 34–43). Jesus spoke of many kinds of fish being caught in the same net, with the good being kept and the bad being thrown away (13:47–50). He spoke of houses without foundations (7:24–27), virgins without oil for their lamps, and servants who wasted their talents and so were "cast out" (25:1–30). He warned of gates and paths that seem right, but that lead to destruction (7:13–14).

Some of the Corinthians apparently had intellectually and/or outwardly acknowledged Jesus' lordship, saviorhood, and resurrection, but had not trusted in Him or committed themselves to Him. They believed only as the demons believe (Jas 2:19). They acknowledged Christ, but they had not **received** Him, did not **stand** in Him, were not **saved** by Him, and did not **hold fast** to His **word,** which Paul had **preached** to them. As Jesus made clear in the illustrations just cited above, many people make positive responses of one sort or another to the gospel, but only genuine faith in Jesus Christ results in salvation.

Many people have useless faith. "Many" will say, "Lord, Lord," in the day of judgment, but be excluded because of their empty, sham faith (Matt 7:22–23; 25:11–12). Those who forsake Christ and His church prove that they never really belonged to Him or to

His true Body (cf. 1 John 2:19). It is those who "abide in My word," Jesus said, those who **hold fast the word,** who "are truly disciples of Mine" (John 8:31; cf. 2 Cor 13:5; 2 John 9). The truly justified and righteous not only are saved by faith but continue to "live by faith" (Heb 10:38). Obedience and continuous faithfulness mark the redeemed.

The fact that, despite their great immaturity and many weaknesses, the Corinthian church even continued to exist was a strong testimony to the power of the gospel. Who but the risen, living Christ could have taken extortioners, thieves, adulterers, fornicators, homosexuals, liars, idolaters, and such thoroughly worldly pagans and transformed them into a community of the redeemed? Despite their shortcomings and failures, and despite the presence of false followers in their assembly, Christ lived in and through the true saints. Paul was ashamed of much of what they did and did not do, but he was not ashamed to call them **brethren.**

Though it is largely a subjective proof, the endurance of the church of Jesus Christ through 2,000 years is evidence of His resurrection reality. His church and His Word have survived skepticism, persecution, heresy, unfaithfulness, and disobedience. Critics have denounced the resurrection as a hoax and fabrication, but have never explained the power of such a fabrication to produce men and women who gave up everything, including their freedom and lives when necessary, to love and to follow a dead Lord! His living church is evidence that Christ Himself is alive; and He could be alive only if He had been raised from the dead.

H. D. A. Major, former principal of Ripon Hall, Oxford, has written,

> Had the crucifixion of Jesus ended His disciples' experience of Him, it is hard to see how the Christian Church could have come into existence. That Church was founded on faith in the Messiahship of Jesus. A crucified Messiah was no Messiah at all. He was one rejected by Judaism and accursed of God. It was the Resurrection of Jesus, as St. Paul declares in Rom. 14, which proclaimed Him to be the Son of God with power (*The Mission and Message of Jesus* [New York: Dutton, 1946], 213).

Church historian Kenneth Scott Latourette wrote in *History of the Expansion of Christianity*,

> It was the conviction of the resurrection of Jesus which lifted his followers out of the despair into which his death had cast them and which led to the perpetuation of the movement begun by him. But for their profound belief that the crucified had risen from the dead and they had seen him and talked with him, the death of Jesus and even Jesus himself would probably have been all but forgotten (vol. 1 [New York: Harper & Row, 1970], 59).

A follower of Buddha writes of that religious leader, "When Buddha died it was with that utter passing away in which nothing whatever remains." Mohammed died at Medina on June 8, 632, at the age of sixty-one, and his tomb there is visited yearly by tens of thousands of Muslims. But they come to mourn his death, not to celebrate his resurrection. Yet the church of Jesus Christ, not just on Easter Sunday but at every service of immersion baptism, celebrates the victory of her Lord over death and the grave.

THE TESTIMONY OF SCRIPTURE

For I delivered to you as of first importance what I also received, that Christ died for our sins according to the Scriptures, and that He was buried, and that He was raised on the third day according to the Scriptures. (15:3–4)

The second evidence for Christ's resurrection was the Old Testament, **the Scriptures** of Judaism and of the early church. The Old Testament clearly predicted Christ's death, burial, and resurrection. When Paul says **I delivered to you,** he means he brought authoritative teaching, not something of his own origination. He did not design it, he only **delivered** what God had authored.

To the two disciples on the road to Emmaus, Jesus said, "'O foolish men and slow of heart to believe in all that the prophets have spoken! Was it not necessary for the Christ to suffer these things and to enter into His glory?' And beginning with Moses and with all the prophets, He explained to them the things concerning Himself in all the Scriptures" (Luke 24:25–27). When the unbelieving Jews asked for a sign of Jesus' messiahship, He responded, "An evil and adulterous generation craves for a sign; and yet no sign shall be given to it but the sign of Jonah the prophet; for just as Jonah was three days and three nights in the belly of the sea monster, so shall the Son of Man be three days and three nights in the heart of the earth" (Matt 12:39–40).

At Pentecost, Peter quoted from Psalm 16 and then commented that David, the author of the psalm, "looked ahead and spoke of the resurrection of the Christ, that He was neither abandoned to Hades, nor did His flesh suffer decay" (Acts 2:25–31). Paul proclaimed before King Agrippa, "And so, having obtained help from God, I stand to this day testifying both to small and great, stating nothing but what the Prophets and Moses said was going to take place; that the Christ was to suffer, and that by reason of His resurrection from the dead He should be the first to proclaim light both to the Jewish people and to the Gentiles" (Acts 26:22–23).

Jesus, Peter, and Paul quoted or referred to such Old Testament passages as Genesis 22:8, 14; Psalm 16:8–11; Psalm 22; Isaiah 53; and Hosea 6:2. Over and over again, either directly or indirectly, literally or in figures of speech, the Old Testament foretold Jesus' death, burial, and resurrection. No Jew who believed and understood **the Scriptures,** referring to what we now call the Old Testament, should have been surprised that the Messiah was ordained to die, be buried, and then resurrected. Twice Paul repeats the phrase **according to the Scriptures,** to emphasize that this is no new thing, and no contradiction of true Jewish belief.

THE TESTIMONY OF EYEWITNESSES

And that He appeared to Cephas, then to the twelve. After that He appeared to more than five hundred brethren at one time, most of whom remain until now, but some have fallen asleep; then He appeared to James, then to all the apostles. (15:5–7)

Throughout history, the testimony of responsible and honest eyewitnesses has been considered one of the most reliable forms of evidence in a court of law. Paul's third evidence for Christ's resurrection is in that form.

Lawyer Sir Edward Clarke said,

As a lawyer I have made a prolonged study of the evidences for the events of the first Easter day. For me, the evidence is conclusive, and over and over again in the high court I have secured the verdict on evidence not nearly so compelling. Inference follows on evidence, and a truthful witness is always artless and disdains effect; the gospel evidence for the resurrection is of this class, and as a lawyer I accept it unreservedly as the testimony of truthful men to facts they were able to substantiate.

The historian Thomas Arnold of Oxford has written,

The evidence for our Lord's life and death and resurrection may be and often has been shown to be satisfactory. It is good according to the common rules for distinguishing good evidence from bad. Thousands and tens of thousands of persons have gone through it piece by piece as carefully as every judge summing up on an important case. I have myself done it many times over, not to persuade others but to satisfy myself. I have been used for many years to study the history of other times, and to examine and weigh the evidence of those who have written about them, and I know of no one fact in the history of mankind which is better proved by fuller evidence than the great sign that God has given us that Christ died and rose again from the dead.

JESUS' APPEARANCE TO PETER

It is significant that Paul says that Jesus **appeared** to those who saw Him after the resurrection. Until He revealed His identity to them, not even Mary Magdelene (John 20:14–16), the two disciples on the Emmaus road (Luke 24:15, 31), or the disciples gathered together on Easter evening (John 20:19–20) recognized Him. The gospel accounts consistently speak of Jesus' appearing or manifesting Himself after His resurrection

(Matt 28:9; Mark 16:9, 12, 14; Luke 24:31–39; John 21:1; etc.). He was recognized only by those to whom He chose to reveal Himself, and there is no record that He revealed Himself to any other than His followers.

One of the requirements for apostleship was having seen the resurrected Christ (Acts 1:22), and the first apostle to whom **He appeared** was **Cephas,** that is, Peter. We are not told the exact time or occasion for that appearance. We only know that it was sometime after His appearance to Mary and before His appearance to the two disciples on the road to Emmaus (Luke 24:34). We are not told why the Lord appeared to Peter first or separately, but it possibly was because of Peter's great remorse over having denied his Lord, and because of his role as a leader among the apostles and in the primitive church until the Council of Jerusalem (Acts 15). In going to Peter first, Jesus emphasized His grace. Peter had forsaken the Lord, but the Lord had not forsaken him. Christ did not appear to Peter because Peter deserved to see Him most, but perhaps because Peter needed to see Him most. Peter was the Lord's spokesman at Pentecost and was crucially used in the expansion of the church for several years. As such he was the prime witness to the resurrected Christ.

JESUS' APPEARANCE TO THE TWELVE

Jesus next appeared **to the twelve.** As mentioned above, He appeared to the eleven disciples (though still often referred to as "the twelve" even before Judas was replaced) as they were fearfully assembled on Easter evening (John 20:19; Luke 24:36).

The apostles laid the foundation of the church (Eph 2:20), which from the beginning based its beliefs and practices on their teaching (Acts 2:42). Those men whom the Lord used to establish His church on earth all saw Him in His resurrected body (Acts 1:22). They were capable, honest, and reliable witnesses to the most important event of history.

JESUS' APPEARANCE TO THE FIVE HUNDRED

After that He appeared to more than five hundred brethren at one time. The quality of specific witnesses is represented by the apostles, all of whom were known by name and could easily be questioned. The quantity of witnesses is seen in the **five hundred brethren** who all saw the risen Christ **at one time.** Scripture gives no indication of who those people were, or where Jesus appeared to them, but they were surely well known in the early church, and, like the twelve, would often have been questioned about seeing the risen Savior. Even at the time of Paul's writing, more than two decades later, most of the witnesses were still alive. They

remain until now, he adds, **but some have fallen asleep,** that is, died.

At the same time and same place, five hundred witnesses saw Jesus alive after His resurrection!

JESUS' APPEARANCE TO JAMES

We are not told to which **James** Christ **then ... appeared.** Two of the apostles, one the son of Zebedee and the other the son of Alphaeus, were named James (Mark 3:17–18). I am inclined to believe, however, that this James was the half-brother of the Lord, the author of the letter of James and a key leader in the Jerusalem church (Acts 15:13–21).

James originally was a skeptic. Like his brothers he did not at first believe that Jesus was the Messiah (John 7:5). But now this member of Jesus' own household, this one who for several years did not recognize Jesus as the Christ, was a witness, a powerful and convincing witness, to His resurrection. Perhaps, as with Paul, it was the experience of seeing the resurrected Christ that finally brought **James** to saving faith. In any case, the convincing testimony of a family member and former unbeliever was added to that of the apostles and the five hundred.

"Over a period of forty days" (Acts 1:3), between His resurrection and ascension, Jesus appeared **to all the apostles** on other occasions that are not specified (see John 21:1–14).

THE TESTIMONY OF A SPECIAL WITNESS

And last of all, as it were to one untimely born, He appeared to me also. For I am the least of the apostles, who am not fit to be called an apostle, because I persecuted the church of God. But by the grace of God I am what I am, and His grace toward me did not prove vain; but I labored even more than all of them, yet not I, but the grace of God with me. (15:8–10)

The fourth major testimony of Christ's resurrection was that of the apostle Paul himself, a special and unique witness of the risen Lord. Paul was not among the original apostles, all of whom had been disciples of Jesus during His earthly ministry. He was not among the five hundred other believers who had seen the resurrected Christ. Rather, he had for many years been an unbeliever and a chief persecutor of the church.

He was, however, **last of all** allowed to see the risen Christ. The Lord's appearance to Paul not only was postresurrection but postascension, making Paul's testimony more unique still. It was not during the forty days in which He appeared to all the others but several years later. All the others to whom Christ appeared, except perhaps James, were believers, whereas Paul (then known as Saul) was a violent, hateful unbeliever when the Lord manifested Himself on the Damascus road (Acts 9:1–8). There were also other appearances (Acts 18:9–10; 23:11; cf. 2 Cor 12:1–7).

Jesus appeared to Paul **as it were to one untimely born.** *Ektrōma* (**untimely born**) ordinarily referred to an abortion, miscarriage, or premature birth—a life unable to sustain itself. In Paul's figure, the term could indicate hopelessness for life without divine intervention, and convey the idea that he was born without hope of meeting Christ. But the use of the term in the sense of an ill-timed birth, too early or too late, seems to fit Paul's thought best. He came too late to have been one of the twelve. In carrying the idea of unformed, dead, and useless, the term was also used as a term of derision. Before his conversion, which coincided with his vision of the resurrected Lord, Paul was spiritually unformed, dead, and useless, a person to be scorned by God. Even when he was born it was wrong timing. Christ was gone. How could he be an apostle? Yet, by special divine provision, **He appeared to me also,** Paul testifies.

Though Paul never doubted his apostleship or hesitated to use the authority that office brought, he also never ceased to be amazed that, of all persons, Christ would have called him to that high position. He not only considered himself to be **the least of the apostles,** but not even **fit to be called an apostle, because** [he] **persecuted the church of God.**

Paul knew all of his sins were forgiven, and he was not plagued by feelings of guilt over what he had once done against God's people. But he could not forget that for which he had been forgiven, and it continually reminded him that **by the grace of God I am what I am.** That he deserved God's forgiveness so little was a constant reminder of how graciously His grace is given.

It is possible that Paul's memory of having **persecuted the church of God** was a powerful motivation for his being determined that **His grace would not prove vain.** (Compare his testimony in 1 Tim 1:12–17.) As is clearly substantiated in the New Testament, Paul was able to truthfully say, **I labored even more than all of them.** (Compare his commitment as chronicled in 2 Cor 11:23–12:12.) Yet he was not boasting in his own spirituality or power but in God's, because, as he hastened to add, **yet not I, but the grace of God with me.** The same grace responsible for his calling was responsible for his faithfulness. God sovereignly appointed Paul an apostle and sovereignly blessed his apostolic ministry. Paul believed, responded, obeyed, and was continually sensitive to the Lord's leading and will. But apart from God's prevenient grace, the apostle knew that everything he did would have been in vain and worthless (cf. Eph 4:15–16; Col 1:28–29; etc.).

The truth and power of the resurrected Christ had brought three great changes in Paul. First was deep recognition of sin. For the first time, he realized how far his external religious life was from being internally godly. He saw himself as he really was, an enemy of God and a persecutor of His church. Second, he experienced a revolution of character. From a persecutor of the church he became her greatest defender. His life was transformed from one characterized by self-righteous hatred to one characterized by self-giving love. He changed from oppressor to servant, from imprisoner to deliverer, from judge to friend, from a taker of life to a giver of life. Third, he experienced a dramatic redirection of energy. As zealously as he had once opposed God's redeemed, he now served them.

THE TESTIMONY OF THE COMMON MESSAGE

Whether then it was I or they, so we preach and so you believed. (15:11)

The last testimony to Christ's resurrection was that of the common message that every true apostle, prophet, and pastor preached. **Whether then it was I or they**—Peter, the twelve, the five hundred, James, or anyone else—**so we preach and so you believed.** Without exception, the preaching and teaching in the early church centered on the death, burial, and resurrection of Christ. Wherever Christ was preached and by whomever He was preached, His resurrection was the pivotal message that was proclaimed. There was no dispute about the truth or the importance of the doctrine, which hardly would have been the case had it been a fabrication.

Except for a few isolated heresies, the doctrine of Christ's resurrection has not been questioned within the church until our modern age of skepticism and humanism. New Testament Christianity, whether ancient or modern, knows nothing of a gospel whose heart is not the risen Lord and Savior, Jesus Christ.

02

THE IMPORTANCE OF BODILY RESURRECTION

1 CORINTHIANS 15:12–19

Now if Christ is preached, that He has been raised from the dead, how do some among you say that there is no resurrection of the dead? But if there is no resurrection of the dead, not even Christ has been raised; and if Christ has not been raised, then our preaching is vain, your faith also is vain. Moreover we are even found to be false witnesses of God, because we witnessed against God that He raised Christ, whom He did not raise, if in fact the dead are not raised. For if the dead are not raised, not even Christ has been raised; and if Christ has not been raised, your faith is worthless; you are still in your sins. Then those also who have fallen asleep in Christ have perished. If we have hoped in Christ in this life only, we are of all men most to be pitied. (15:12–19)

As Paul reminded them in verses 1–11, the Corinthian Christians already believed in Christ's resurrection, else they would not have been Christians. That affirmation of the reality of the resurrection formed the basis for his double-edged argument in chapter 15: Because Christ was raised, resurrection from the dead obviously is possible; and, on the other hand, unless men in general can be resurrected, Christ could not have been raised. The two resurrections stand or fall together; there could not be one without the other. Furthermore, if there is no resurrection, the gospel is meaningless and worthless.

It seems strange that some of those believers could have accepted one part of the truth without the other. The cause of this confusion, as of many of their other problems, lay in the continuing influence of the pagan philosophies and religions out of which many of them had come. The philosophical and spiritualistic thought of Paul's day, just as in our own, had many erroneous ideas of what happens to human beings after death.

Some religions have taught soul sleep, in which the body dies and disintegrates, while the soul or spirit rests. Materialists believe in utter extinction, total annihilation. Nothing human, physical or otherwise, survives after death. Death ends it all. Some religions teach reincarnation, wherein the soul or spirit is continually recycled from one form to another—even from human to animal or animal to human. Others believe in what is generally described as absorption, in which the spirit, or at least a certain part of the spirit, returns back to its source and is absorbed back into the ultimate divine mind or being. That belief is reflected in a statement of the contemporary philosopher Leslie Weatherhead: "Would it really matter if I were lost like a drop of water in the ocean, if I could be one shining particle in some glorious wave that broke in utter splendour in perfect beauty on the shores of some eternal sea?"

In all those views, human personhood and individuality are forever lost at death. Whatever, if anything, survives is no longer a person, no longer an individual, no longer a unique being.

A basic tenet of much ancient Greek philosophy was dualism, a concept generally attributed to Plato. Dualism considered everything spiritual to be intrinsically good and everything physical to be intrinsically evil. To anyone holding that view, the idea of a resurrected body was repugnant. For them, the very reason for going to an afterlife was to escape all things physical. They considered the body a tomb or a corpse, to which, in this life, their souls were shackled. For those Greeks, their bodies were the last things they would want to take along to the next life. They believed in the immortality of the soul but strongly opposed the idea of a resurrection of the body—as Paul had experienced when he preached on the Areopagus: "Now when they [the Athenian philosophers] heard of the resurrection of the dead, some began to sneer" (Acts 17:32). The typical view of dualism was expressed by Seneca: "When the day shall come which shall part this mixture of divine and human here where I found it, I will leave my body, and myself I will give back to the gods."

It is possible that even some of the Jewish members of the Corinthian church doubted the resurrection. Despite the fact that resurrection is taught in the Old

Testament, some Jews, such as the Sadducees, did not believe in it.

In the ancient book of Job we read, "Even after my skin is destroyed, yet from my flesh I shall see God" (Job 19:26; cf. Ps 17:15). Ezekiel's vision of the dry bones (37:1–14) pictures the restored nation of Israel but also suggests the bodily resurrection of God's people. Daniel's prediction of resurrection is clear, speaking of the resurrection of the lost as well as of the saved. "And many of those who sleep in the dust of the ground will awake, these to everlasting life, but the others to disgrace and everlasting contempt" (Dan 12:2).

But whereas the Old Testament teaching about the resurrection was limited and incomplete, the New Testament teaching is extensive. Though the gospels were not yet written, Jesus' life was well known and the Corinthians doubtless had learned of His teaching from Peter and others. "No one can come to Me unless the Father who sent Me draws him; and I will raise him up on the last day" (John 6:44), He proclaimed to some of His Jewish critics near the Sea of Galilee. To Martha He said, "I am the resurrection and the life; he who believes in Me shall live even if he dies" (John 11:25).

The foundation of apostolic teaching was that Christ rose from the dead and that all who believed in Him would also be raised. As Peter and John were preaching in Jerusalem soon after Pentecost, "the priests and the captain of the temple guard, and the

Sadducees, came upon them, being greatly disturbed because they were teaching the people and proclaiming in Jesus the resurrection from the dead" (Acts 4:1–2). Paul had written the Thessalonians several years before he wrote 1 Corinthians, "For the Lord Himself will descend from heaven with a shout, with the voice of the archangel, and with the trumpet of God; and the dead in Christ shall rise first" (1 Thess 4:16). He doubtlessly had taught the Corinthians the same truth, and in his next letter to them he says, "He who raised the Lord Jesus will raise us also with Jesus and will present us with you" (2 Cor 4:14).

In spite of the fact that the resurrection of believers is taught in the Old Testament, in the teaching of Jesus during His earthly ministry, and in the teaching of the apostles, serious doubts about it had infected many of the Corinthian Christians. It is those doubts that Paul forcefully counters in 1 Corinthians 15.

His first argument is simple and logical: **Now if Christ is preached, that He has been raised from the dead, how do some among you say that there is no resurrection of the dead?** The construction here (*ei* with the indicative) implies a condition that is true. The Corinthians believed in Christ's resurrection (1 Cor 15:1, 11) and that He was presently alive (emphasized by the perfect tense of *egeirō*, **has been raised**). How then could they logically deny the general truth of resurrection? If Christ has been raised, resurrection obviously is possible.

In verses 13–19 the apostle demonstrates that the resurrection is not only possible but essential to the faith, by giving seven disastrous consequences, four theological and three personal, that would result if there were no resurrection: (1) Christ would not be risen; (2) preaching of the gospel would be meaningless; (3) faith in Christ would be worthless; (4) all witnesses to and all preachers of the resurrection would be liars; (5) all men would still be in their sins; (6) all former believers would have eternally perished; and (7) Christians would be the most pitiable people on earth.

THE THEOLOGICAL CONSEQUENCES OF NO RESURRECTION

But if there is no resurrection of the dead, not even Christ has been raised; and if Christ has not been raised, then our preaching is vain, your faith also is vain. Moreover we are even found to be false witnesses of God, because we witnessed against God that He raised Christ, whom He did not raise, if in fact the dead are not raised. (15:13–15)

CHRIST WOULD NOT BE RISEN

The first and most obvious consequence of there being no resurrection would be that **not even**

Christ has been raised. "As anyone should easily deduce," Paul argues, "if the dead cannot rise, Christ did not rise."

It is likely that the disbelieving Corinthians got around that problem by claiming that Christ was not really a man, or was not fully a man. Because of their dualistic orientation, as discussed above, they assumed that because Christ was divine He could not possibly have been human, and therefore only appeared to be human. Consequently He did not really die but only appeared to die. According to this view, His appearances between the crucifixion (an illusion) and the ascension were simply continuing manifestations that only seemed to be bodily.

That view, of course, cannot square with what the gospel writers, Jesus Himself, and the apostles taught. The gospel accounts of Jesus' earthly life and ministry are of a person who was entirely human. He was born to a human mother, and He ate, drank, slept, became tired, was crucified, was stabbed, bled, and died. At His first appearance to the twelve after the crucifixion, Jesus made a point of having the disciples touch Him in order to prove that He was not simply a spirit, which "does not have flesh and bones as you see that I have." He next asked for something to eat and then "took it and ate it before them" (Luke 24:39–43).

At Pentecost, Peter proclaimed that "Jesus the Nazarene [was] a man attested to you by God" and that "this Man delivered up by the predetermined plan and foreknowledge of God, you nailed to a cross" (Acts 2:22–23). Later in the same message he proclaimed that Jesus was still alive, not merely in spirit but in body. He told of David's speaking "of the resurrection of the Christ, that He was neither abandoned to Hades, nor did His flesh suffer decay. This Jesus God raised up again" (Acts 2:31–32). In his opening words to the Romans, Paul makes it clear that "the gospel of God" for which he was set apart was "concerning His Son, who was born of a descendant of David according to the flesh, who was declared the Son of God with power by the resurrection from the dead" (Rom 1:1–4). Jesus' resurrection evidenced both His humanity and His deity.

In His vision to John on Patmos, Christ declared, "I am the first and the last, and the living One; and I was dead, and behold, I am alive forevermore, and I have the keys of death and of Hades" (Rev 1:17–18). In his second letter John points up the crucial importance of believing that Jesus was born, lived, died, and was raised up a human being: "For many deceivers have gone out into the world, those who do not acknowledge Jesus Christ as coming in the flesh. This is the deceiver and the antichrist" (2 John 7).

The Corinthians could not fall back on the pagan notion that Christ only appeared to be human. He was fully human; He physically lived and died and lived again. Therefore, if there is no such thing as physical resurrection, **not even Christ has been raised.**

PREACHING OF THE GOSPEL WOULD BE MEANINGLESS

The second consequence of there being no resurrection would be that **preaching** of the gospel would be **vain,** completely meaningless. As Paul had just said, the heart of the gospel is Christ's death and resurrection on our behalf. "For I delivered to you as of first importance what I also received, that Christ died for our sins according to the Scriptures, and that He was buried, and that He was raised on the third day according to the Scriptures" (15:3–4). Apart from the resurrection, Jesus could not have conquered sin or death or hell, and those three great evils would forever be man's conquerors.

Without the resurrection, the good news would be bad news, and there would be nothing worth preaching. Without the resurrection, the gospel would be an empty, hopeless message of meaningless nonsense. Unless our Lord conquered sin and death, making a way for men to follow in that victory, there is no gospel to proclaim.

FAITH IN CHRIST WOULD BE WORTHLESS

Just as no resurrection would make preaching Christ meaningless, it would also make faith in Him worthless. Faith in such a gospel would be **vain** (*kenos*, empty, fruitless, void of effect, to no purpose). A dead savior could not give life. If the dead do not rise, Christ did not rise and we will not rise. We then could only say with the psalmist, "Surely in vain I have kept my heart pure" (Ps 73:13), or with the Servant in Isaiah, "I have toiled in vain, I have spent My strength for nothing and vanity" (Isa 49:4).

If there were no resurrection, the hall of the faithful in Hebrews 11 would instead be the hall of the foolish. Abel, Enoch, Noah, Abraham, Sarah, Moses, Rahab, David, the prophets, and all the others would have been faithful for nothing. They would have been mocked, scourged, imprisoned, stoned, afflicted, ill-treated, and put to death completely in **vain.** All believers of all ages would have believed for nothing, lived for nothing, and died for nothing.

ALL WITNESSES TO AND PREACHERS OF THE RESURRECTION WOULD BE LIARS

Moreover we are even found to be false witnesses of God, because we witnessed against God that He raised Christ, whom He did not raise, if in fact the dead are not raised. If there is no such thing as resurrection of the dead, then every person who claimed to have witnessed the risen Christ and every person who preached the risen Christ was a liar, including Paul and the other apostles (**we**). They would be pseudo-witnesses, claiming falsely to be from God and witnessing falsely **against** [concerning] **God that He raised Christ.**

To deny the resurrection is to call the apostles and every other leader of the New Testament church not simply mistaken but willfully mistaken, that is, liars. There is no possibility, as many liberals claim, that such a mistake could have been innocent or naive. Those witnesses could not have been honest men who unwittingly gave bad advice. If Christ was not raised from the dead, they not only were not sent by God with a message from Him, but were liars who would have had to conspire together in order for their lies to have been so consistent and harmonized.

If the apostles, the prophets, and the New Testament writers lied about the heart of the gospel, why should they be believed about anything else? Why should their moral teachings be considered inspired and lofty if they so blatantly falsified their teaching about Jesus' resurrection? All New Testament truth stands or falls together based on the resurrection.

Not only that, but those witnesses would have testified, preached, and taught a lie for which they were maligned, beaten, imprisoned, and often martyred. Such self sacrifice, however, is not the stuff of which charlatans are made. People do not die to preserve a lie.

Although Paul does not mention it specifically, it clearly follows that if the resurrection were not true, Christ Himself lied, or at best was tragically mistaken.

In either case, He hardly would have qualified as the divine Son of God or the world's Savior and Lord. Jesus would not have been Victor but victim. Or, if the New Testament writers completely misrepresented what both Christ and the apostles taught, then the New Testament would be a worthless document that no reasonable person would trust.

THE PERSONAL CONSEQUENCES OF NO RESURRECTION

For if the dead are not raised, not even Christ has been raised; and if Christ has not been raised, your faith is worthless; you are still in your sins. Then those also who have fallen asleep in Christ have perished. If we have hoped in Christ in this life only, we are of all men most to be pitied. (15:16–19)

Next Paul gives what may be described as three personal consequences that would result if there were no such thing as resurrection from the dead. Like the other four, these consequences have serious theological significance, but they also state much more directly how believers would be affected.

ALL MEN WOULD STILL BE IN THEIR SINS

In verse 16 Paul restates his major argument: **If the dead are not raised, not even Christ has been**

raised. A dead Christ would be the chief disastrous consequence from which all the other consequences would result.

The next consequence Paul mentions is both personal and serious: **If Christ has not been raised, your faith is worthless; you are still in your sins.** After repeating the consequence that believers' faith would be **worthless,** or vain (v. 14), the apostle points to the obvious additional result that believers would be no better off spiritually than unbelievers. Christians would **still** be in their **sins** just as much as the most wicked and unbelieving pagan. We would all be in the same boat as the unbelievers to whom Jesus said, "You … shall die in your sin" (John 8:21).

If Jesus did not rise from the dead, then sin won the victory over Christ and therefore continues to be victorious over all men. If Jesus remained dead, then, when we die, we too will remain dead and damned. "The wages of sin is death" (Rom 6:23), and if we remain dead, then death and eternal punishment are the only prospects of believer and unbeliever alike. The purpose of trusting in Christ is for forgiveness of sins, because it is from sin that we need to be saved. "Christ died for our sins" and "was buried, and … raised on the third day" (1 Cor 15:3–4). If Christ was not raised, His death was in vain, our faith in Him is in vain, and our sins are still counted against us. We are still dead in trespasses and sins and will forever remain spiritually dead and sinful. If Christ was not raised, then He did not bring forgiveness of sins or salvation or reconciliation or spiritual life, either for now or for eternity.

But God *did* raise "Jesus our Lord from the dead, He who was delivered up because of our transgressions, and was raised because of our justification" (Rom 4:24–25). Because Christ does live, we too shall live (John 14:19). "The God of our fathers raised up Jesus, whom you had put to death by hanging Him on a cross. He is the one whom God exalted to His right hand as a Prince and a Savior, to grant repentance to Israel, and forgiveness of sins" (Acts 5:30–31).

ALL FORMER BELIEVERS WOULD HAVE ETERNALLY PERISHED

If there is no resurrection, **then those also who have fallen asleep in Christ have perished. Fallen asleep** does not refer to what is often called soul sleep but was a common euphemism for death (cf. vv. 6, 20; Matt 27:52; Acts 7:60; 2 Pet 3:4). Every saint, Old Testament or Christian, who had died would have forever **perished.** Obviously the same consequence would apply to every saint who has died since Paul wrote. Paul himself, the other apostles, Augustine, Calvin, Luther, Wesley, D. L. Moody, and every other believer of every other age would spend eternity in torment, without God and without hope. Their faith would have been in vain, their sins would have been unforgiven, and their destiny would be damnation.

CHRISTIANS WOULD BE THE MOST PITIABLE PEOPLE ON EARTH

In light of the other consequences, the last is rather obvious. **If we have hoped in Christ in this life only** [and we have; *ei* with the indicative] **we are of all men most to be pitied.** Without the resurrection, and the salvation and blessings it brings, Christianity would be pointless and pitiable. Without the resurrection we would have no Savior, no forgiveness, no gospel, no meaningful faith, no life, and no hope of any of those things.

To have **hoped in Christ in this life only** would be to teach, preach, suffer, sacrifice, and work entirely for nothing. If Christ is still dead, then He not only cannot help us in regard to the life to come but He cannot help us now. If He cannot grant us eternal life, He cannot improve our earthly life. If He is not alive, where would be our source of peace, joy, or satisfaction now? The Christian life would be a mockery, a charade, a tragic joke.

A Christian has no Savior but Christ, no Redeemer but Christ, no Lord but Christ. Therefore if Christ was not raised, He is not alive, and our Christian life is lifeless. We would have nothing to justify our faith, our Bible study, our preaching or witnessing, our service for Him or our worship of Him, and nothing to justify our hope either for this life or the next. We would deserve nothing but the compassion reserved for fools.

But we are *not* to be pitied, for Paul immediately continues, "But now Christ has been raised from the dead, the first fruits of those who are asleep" (15:20).

03

THE RESURRECTION PLAN

1 CORINTHIANS 15:20-28

But now Christ has been raised from the dead, the first fruits of those who are asleep. For since by a man came death, by a man also came the resurrection of the dead. For as in Adam all die, so also in Christ all shall be made alive. But each in his own order: Christ the first fruits, after that those who are Christ's at His coming, then comes the end, when He delivers up the kingdom to the God and Father, when He has abolished all rule and all authority and power. For He must reign until He has put all His enemies under His feet. The last enemy that will be abolished is death. For He has put all things in subjection under His feet. But when He says, "All things are put in subjection," it is evident that He is excepted who put all things in subjection to Him. And when all things are subjected to Him, then the Son Himself also will be subjected to the One who subjected all things to Him, that God may be all in all. (15:20–28)

Theologian Erich Sauer has written, "The present age is Easter time. It begins with the resurrection of the Redeemer and ends with the resurrection of the redeemed. Between lies the spiritual resurrection of those called into life through Christ. So we live between two Easters, and in the power of the first Easter we go to meet the last Easter." The last Easter to which

Sauer refers is, of course, the bodily resurrection of the saved. Scripture speaks of that resurrection of the righteous (Rev 20:6; 1 Thess 4:13–18; 2 Cor 5:1–5; Luke 14:14; John 5:29), calling it the first resurrection. The second is the resurrection of the unrighteous (John 5:29). It is of the first resurrection that Paul speaks in 1 Corinthians 15.

The apostle has reminded the Corinthians that they already believed in Christ's resurrection (15:1–11) and that logically they must also believe in their own resurrection and that of all saints, mentioning seven disastrous and absurd consequences that would result if they were not raised (vv. 12–19). Moving into verses 20–28 Paul discusses three aspects of the resurrection of the righteous: (1) The Redeemer; (2) the redeemed; and (3) the restoration. The first and third focus on Christ; the second focuses on believers.

THE REDEEMER

But now Christ has been raised from the dead, the first fruits of those who are asleep. For since by a man came death, by a man also came the resurrection of the dead. For as in Adam all die, so also in Christ all shall be made alive. (15:20–22)

First, Paul reaffirms Christ's resurrection: **But now Christ has been raised from the dead,** a truth his readers already acknowledged and believed (vv. 1–2). The words "and become," found in some translations (e.g., the KJV), do not come first in the original text and are misleading. Christ did not become the **first fruits** at some time after His resurrection, but at the moment of His resurrection, by the very fact of His resurrection. His being raised made Him the first fruits of all who would be raised.

Before Israelites harvested their crops, they were to bring a representative sample, called the first fruits, to the priests as an offering to the Lord (Lev 23:10). The full harvest could not be made until the first fruits were offered. That is the point of Paul's figure here. Christ's own resurrection was the **first fruits** of the resurrection "harvest" of the believing dead. In His death and resurrection, Christ made an offering of Himself to the Father on our behalf.

The significance of the first fruits, however, not only was that they preceded the harvest but that they were a first installment of the harvest. The fact that Christ was **the first fruits** therefore indicates that something else, namely the harvest of the rest of the crop, is to follow. In other words, Christ's resurrection could not have been in isolation from ours. His resurrection *requires* our resurrection, because His resurrection was part of the larger resurrection of God's redeemed.

The resurrection of which Paul speaks here is permanent resurrection. Both the Old and New

Testaments tell of persons who died and were miraculously brought back to life (1 Kings 17:22; 2 Kings 4:34–36; 13:21; Luke 7:15; John 11:44). But all of those persons died again. Even those whom Jesus raised—the son of the widow of Nain, Jairus's daughter, and Lazarus—eventually died again. Christ Himself, however, was the first to be raised never to die again.

As in 15:6, 18 (cf. Matt 27:52; Acts 7:60; 2 Pet 3:4), **those who are asleep** refers to the dead, in this instance to the righteous dead, whose spirits have gone to be with the Lord (2 Cor 5:8; cf. Phil 1:23) but whose remains are in the grave, awaiting recomposition and resurrection.

Through Christ, as a **man, came the resurrection of the dead,** just as through Adam, the first **man, came death.** Paul's point here is that Jesus' humanness was inextricably involved both in His resurrection and in ours. It was because Jesus died, was buried, and was raised as a **man** that He could become the **first fruits** of all other men who would be raised to glory. As already noted, the first fruits and the harvest were from the same crop.

In verse 22 Paul continues to explain how the great truth of the one resurrection of Christ affects believers. The convincing analogy comes from the first man: **For as in Adam all die, so also in Christ all shall be made alive.** Just as Adam was the progenitor of everyone who dies, so Christ is the progenitor of everyone who will be raised to life. In each case, one man doing one act caused the consequences of that act to be applied to every other person identified with him. Those who are identified with Adam—every person who has been born—is subject to death because of Adam's sinful act. Likewise, those who are identified with Christ—every person who has been born again in Him—is subject to resurrection to eternal life because of Christ's righteous act. **In Adam all** have inherited a sin nature and therefore will **die. In Christ all** who believe in Him have inherited eternal life, and **shall be made alive,** in body as well as in spirit. "For as through the one man's disobedience the many were made sinners, even so through the obedience of the One the many will be made righteous" (Rom 5:19).

From countless other passages of Scripture we know that the two **all**s in verse 22, though alike in some respects, cannot be equal. Those who attempt to read universalism into this passage must contradict those other passages that teach reprobation (Matt 5:29; 10:28; 25:41, 46; Luke 16:23; 2 Thess 1:9; Rev 20:15; etc.). The **all**s are alike in that they both apply to descendants. Every human being is a descendant of Adam, and therefore the first **all** is universal. With only the exceptions of Enoch and Elijah, whom the Lord took directly to be with Himself, and of those saints who will be raptured, every person born will die.

Only those who trust in Jesus Christ, however, are *His* descendants (as illustrated in John 8:44), and the second **all** therefore applies only to the saved. It is only **all** the fellow sons of God and joint heirs with Jesus Christ (Gal 3:26, 29; 4:7; Eph 3:6; cf. Acts 20:32; Titus 3:7) who **shall be made alive. In Adam** is simply to be human, to have been born once. **In Christ** is to have eternal life, to be born again. By natural descent from Adam, having inherited his sin, **all die.** By supernatural descent from Christ, having inherited His righteousness, **all shall be made alive.**

Though the inheritance in both cases is bodily as well as spiritual, Paul's major emphasis here is on the bodily. Through Adam's sin, man died spiritually and became subject to death bodily. Likewise, through Christ believers are given life spiritually and will be raised bodily. But our spirits, because they go to be with the Lord at death, will not wait to be resurrected. Only our bodies will be resurrected, and that is the truth stressed here.

THE REDEEMED

But each in his own order: Christ the first fruits, after that those who are Christ's at His coming. (15:23)

In the scheme of resurrection, **Christ** is **the first fruits** and **those who are Christ's at His coming** are the full harvest. Unlike the grain harvest, however, that of the resurrection is far removed in time from the **first fruits.** We do not know—in fact, are told we cannot know (Matt 24:36, 42, 44, 50; 25:13)—when the Lord will come to raise and rapture His people and set up His kingdom. We do not know the time, the specific generation or moment, but we know the **order.**

Most obvious is that Christ was **first** and that our resurrection will follow at **His coming.** From other parts of Scripture we learn that even the "harvest" will not be all at once, but will have its own **order,** its own sequence. The first resurrection has two major parts—Christ's resurrection and believers' resurrection. The resurrection of believers, **those who are Christ's,** will be in three stages, according to different groups of believers.

Initially will be the resurrection of the church, those believers who will have come to saving faith from Pentecost to the rapture. "For the Lord Himself will descend from heaven with a shout, with the voice of the archangel, and with the trumpet of God; and the dead in Christ shall rise first" (1 Thess 4:16). They will be joined by living saints to meet the Lord in the air and ascend to heaven.

Next will be the resurrection of the Tribulation saints. Many will come to trust in Christ during the

Tribulation, that unimaginably horrible seven-year ordeal during which many godly people will be put to death for their faith. At the end of that period, however, all those who will have come to faith in Christ will be raised up to reign with Him during the Millennium (Rev 20:4).

Following that will be the resurrection of Old Testament saints, promised by the prophet Daniel: "And many of those who sleep in the dust of the ground will awake, these to everlasting life, but the others to disgrace and everlasting contempt" (Dan 12:2; cf. Isa 26:19–20). That resurrection, I believe, will occur simultaneously with that of the Tribulation saints.

Then during the millennial kingdom there will, of necessity, be the resurrection of those who die during that time. It is interesting to think that they may well be raised as soon as they die, no burial being necessary. It would make death for a believer during the kingdom nothing more than an instant transformation into his eternal body and spirit.

The only resurrection remaining will be that of the unrighteous, who will be raised to damnation and eternal punishment at the end of Christ's thousand-year reign (John 5:29). The saved will have been raised to eternal life, but the unsaved will be raised to eternal death, the second death (Rev 21:8; cf. 2:11).

THE RESTORATION

Then comes the end, when He delivers up the kingdom to the God and Father, when He has abolished all rule and all authority and power. For He must reign until He has put all His enemies under His feet. The last enemy that will be abolished is death. For He has put all things in subjection under His feet. But when He says, "All things are put in subjection," it is evident that He is excepted who put all things in subjection to Him. And when all things are subjected to Him, then the Son Himself also will be subjected to the One who subjected all things to Him, that God may be all in all. (15:24–28)

The third aspect of the resurrection plan that Paul discusses here is what may be called the restoration. The apostle summarizes some of the things that will happen in the last times.

Then (*eita*, "after this") may imply an interval of time between the resurrection at His coming and the establishment of His kingdom. That would coincide with the teaching of our Lord in Matthew 24 and 25, where He tells of all the signs that will precede His kingdom, even the sign of the Son of Man in heaven and the gathering together of the elect (24:30–31).

Telos (**end**) not only can refer to that which is final but also to that which is completed, consummated, or fulfilled. In the final culmination of the ages, **when He delivers up the kingdom to the God and Father,** all things will be restored as they were originally designed and created by God to be. In the end it will be as it was in the beginning. Sin will be no more, and God will reign supremely, without enemy and without challenge. That gives us great insight into the divine redemptive plan. Here is the culmination: Christ turns over the restored world to God His Father, who sent Him to recover it.

Christ's final act will be to conquer permanently every **enemy** of God, every contending **rule** and **authority** and **power.** They will forever be abolished, never to exist again, never again to oppose God or to deceive, mislead, or threaten His people or corrupt any of His creation.

This final act of Christ, the turning over the world to His Father, will be worked out over the period of a thousand years, during the millennial rule of Christ on earth. As vividly and dramatically portrayed in the symbols and statements of Revelation 5–20, Christ will take back to Himself the earth that He created and that is rightfully His. The scene of Revelation 5 depicts the Son taking rightful possession of the title deed to the earth, His going out to take it back from the usurper to present it to the Father. In doing that, He will quell all rebellions and subdue all enemies. **He must reign until He has put all His enemies under His feet.** It is necessary for Him to rule.

The figure of putting **His enemies under His feet** comes from the common practice in ancient times of kings and emperors always sitting enthroned above their subjects, so that when the subjects bowed they were literally under, or lower than, the sovereign's feet. With enemies, a king often would literally put his foot on the neck of the conquered king or general, symbolizing the enemy's total subjection. In His millennial reign, all of Christ's **enemies** will be put in subjection to Him, **under His feet,** so that God's sovereign plan may be fulfilled.

During the Millennium, no open rebellion will be tolerated, but there will still be rebelliousness in the hearts of Christ's enemies. Because His enemies will not submit to Him willingly, He will have to "rule them with a rod of iron" (Rev 19:15). But they *will be ruled*. At the end of the thousand years Satan will be unleashed for a brief period to lead a final insurrection against God and His kingdom (20:7–9), after which he, with all who belong to him, will be banished to hell, to suffer eternally in the lake of fire (Rev 20:10–15).

The last enemy, both of God and of man, **is death,** which, with all the other enemies, **will be abolished.** Christ broke the power of Satan, "him who had the power of death" (Heb 2:14), at the cross, but Satan and death will not be permanently **abolished** until the end of the Millennium. The victory was won at Calvary, but the eternal peace and righteousness that victory guarantees will not be consummated and completed until the enemies who were conquered are also banished and **abolished.** Then, His final work having been accomplished, Christ **delivers up the kingdom to the God and Father.**

When He took the assignment of salvation from His Father, Christ came to earth as a baby, and lived and grew up as a man among men. He taught, preached, healed, and did miraculous works. He died, was buried, was raised and ascended to His Father, where He now intercedes for those who are His. When He returns He will fight, conquer, rule, judge, and then, as His last work on the Father's behalf, forever subdue and finally judge all the enemies of God (Rev 20:11–15), re-create the earth and heavens (21:1–2), and finally deliver **the kingdom to the God and Father.**

The **kingdom** that Christ **delivers up** will be a redeemed environment indwelt by His redeemed people, those who have become eternal subjects of the everlasting kingdom through faith in Him. In light of Paul's major argument in this chapter, it is obvious that his point here is that, if there were no resurrection, there would be no subjects for God's eternal kingdom; and there would be no Lord to rule. Unless He and they were raised, all of God's people eventually would die, and that would be the end—the end of them and the end of the kingdom. But Scripture assures us that "His kingdom will have no end" (Luke 1:33), and He and His subjects will have no end.

Lest any of his readers misunderstand, Paul goes on to explain the obvious: **But when He says, "All things are put in subjection," it is evident that He is excepted who put all things in subjection to Him.** God the Father is the exception who will not be subject to Christ, for it is the Father who gave the rule and authority to the Son (Matt 28:18; John 5:27), and whom the Son faithfully and perfectly served.

From the time of His incarnation until the time when He presents the kingdom to the Father, Christ is in the role of a Servant, fulfilling His divine task as assigned by His Father. But when that final work is accomplished, He will assume His former, full, glorious place in the perfect harmony of the Trinity. **And when all things are subjected to Him, then the Son Himself also will be subjected to the One who subjected all things to Him, that God may be all in all.** Christ will continue to reign, because His reign is eternal (Rev 11:15), but He will reign with the Father in trinitarian glory, subject to the Trinity in that way eternally designed for Him.

When God created man, He made him perfect, righteous, good, and subservient. At the Fall, this supreme creature of God, along with all the rest of His creation, was corrupted and ruined. But the new men He creates through His Son will never be corrupted or ruined. They will be raised up to live and reign eternally in His eternal kingdom with His eternal Son.

04

RESURRECTION INCENTIVES

1 CORINTHIANS 15:29-34

Otherwise, what will those do who are baptized for the dead? If the dead are not raised at all, why then are they baptized for them? Why are we also in danger every hour? I protest, brethren, by the boasting in you, which I have in Christ Jesus our Lord, I die daily. If from human motives I fought with wild beasts at Ephesus, what does it profit me? If the dead are not raised, Let us eat and drink, for tomorrow we die. Do not be deceived: "Bad company corrupts good morals." Become sober-minded as you ought, and stop sinning; for some have no knowledge of God. I speak this to your shame. (15:29–34)

When the Sadducees, who did not believe in resurrection, asked Jesus the mocking and insincere question about whose wife a certain woman would be in the resurrection, He first told them that they understood neither the Scriptures nor the power of God. After declaring that there is no marriage in heaven, He continued, "But regarding the resurrection of the dead, have you not read that which was spoken to you by God, saying, 'I am the God of Abraham, and the God of Isaac, and the God of Jacob'? He is not the God of the dead but of the living" (Matt 22:23–32; Exod 3:6). The emphasis in His statement was on the verb tense ("I am"). Abraham, Isaac, and Jacob were spiritually alive at the time Jesus spoke, and one day would be reunited with their glorified bodies in the resurrection. He was saying, in effect, "Presently, right now; I am the God of Abraham, Isaac, and Jacob." That was true because there is life after death.

Scripture is not theoretical, impractical, or irrelevant. Because the Sadducees denied resurrection, they could not think or live right, as is obvious in their response to the life and work of Christ. Right doctrine is inseparably connected to right moral behavior; right principles are given to lead to right conduct. God's truth not only is to be believed but properly responded to. We should live the words we love to sing, "Trust and obey, for there's no other way, to be happy in Jesus than to trust and obey." Scriptural truth is not something God gave just to be discussed by theologians and written into creeds. He gave it to be lived out. When its truth is denied, there are devastating moral and spiritual consequences.

The first eleven chapters of Romans are almost pure doctrine, pure theology. Chapter 12 begins, "I urge you therefore, brethren, by the mercies of God, to present your bodies a living and holy sacrifice, acceptable to God, which is your spiritual service of worship" (v. 1). From this point on in the letter, the apostle's teaching is primarily practical, a series of exhortations based on the preceding truths. The "therefore" means "because." "Because of what I have just said, this is the way you should live." Paul echoes the psalmist who wrote, "What shall I render to the Lord for all His benefits toward me?" (Ps 116:12). In Paul's writings, as in Scripture in general, believers' behavior and morality are built on the foundation of God's redemptive work. What God has done is the greatest possible motive for our doing what He wants us to do. To deny the resurrection is, in effect, to deny the need for righteous conduct.

Paul's major thrust in 15:29–34 is: if you remove the resurrection, if you deny this crucial and wonderful truth of God's redemptive work, you have removed one of the greatest motivations the Lord gives for coming to Christ and for living for Christ. He therefore points out three powerful incentives the resurrection gives: (1) an incentive for salvation; (2) an incentive for service; and (3) an incentive for sanctification. The first is for unbelievers, the other two are for believers.

AN INCENTIVE FOR SALVATION

Otherwise, what will those do who are baptized for the dead? If the dead are not raised at all, why then are they baptized for them? (15:29)

This verse is one of the most difficult in all of Scripture, and has many legitimate possible interpretations; it has also, however, been used to support many strange and heretical ideas. The careful and honest interpreter may survey the several dozen interpretations offered and still not be dogmatic about what it means. But we can be dogmatic, from the clear teaching of other parts of Scripture, about some of the things it does *not* mean. As to what this verse does mean, we can only guess, since history has locked it into obscurity.

We can be sure, for example, that it does not teach vicarious, or proxy, baptism for the dead, as claimed by ancient gnostic heretics such as Marcion and by the Mormon church today. Paul did not teach that a person who has died can be saved, or helped in any way, by another person's being baptized in his behalf. Baptismal regeneration, the idea that one is saved by being baptized, or that baptism is in some way necessary for salvation, is unscriptural. The idea of vicarious baptismal regeneration is still further removed from biblical truth. If a person cannot save himself by being baptized, he certainly cannot save anyone else through that act. Salvation is by personal faith in Jesus Christ alone. "For by grace you have been saved through faith; and that not of yourselves, it is the gift of God" (Eph 2:8; cf. Rom 3:28; etc.). That is the repeated and consistent teaching of both the Old and New Testaments. Quoting from Genesis 15:6, Paul says, "For what does the Scripture say? 'And Abraham believed God, and it was reckoned to him as righteousness'" (Rom 4:3). The only way any person has ever come to God is by personal faith.

If one person's faith cannot save another, then certainly one person's baptism cannot save another. Baptism is simply an act of obedient faith that proclaims identity with Christ (Rom 6:3–4). No one is saved by baptism—not even living persons, much less dead ones. "It is appointed for men to die once and after this comes judgment" (Heb 9:27). Death ends all opportunity for salvation and for spiritual help of any sort.

In the New Testament, baptism is closely associated with salvation, of which it is an outward testimony. Although a person does not have to be baptized to be a Christian, he has to be baptized to be an obedient Christian—with the obvious exception of a believer who has no opportunity to be baptized before death. Baptism is an integral part of Christ's Great Commission (Matt 28:19). In the early church, a person who was saved was assumed to have been baptized; and a person was not baptized unless the church was satisfied he was saved. To ask, then, if a person was baptized, was equivalent to asking if he was saved.

If we assume that Paul was using the term *baptized* in that sense, then **those … who are baptized** could refer to those who were giving testimony that they were Christians. In other words, he was simply referring to believers under the title of **those who are baptized,** not to some special act of baptism. **The dead** could also refer to Christians, to deceased believers whose lives were a persuasive testimony leading to the salvation of the **baptized.** This seems to be a reasonable view that does no injustice to the text or context.

The Greek *huper*, translated **for** in verse 29, has a dozen or more meanings, and shades of meaning—including "for," "above," "about," "across," "beyond," "on behalf of," "instead of," "because of," and "in reference to"—depending on grammatical structure and context. Although **for** is a perfectly legitimate translation here, in light of the context and of Paul's clear teaching elsewhere, "because of" could also be a proper rendering.

In light of that reasoning and interpretation, we could guess that Paul may have simply been saying that people were being saved (baptism being the sign) because of the exemplary lives and witness of faithful believers who had died. Whether this is the right interpretation of this verse we cannot be certain, but we can be certain that people often come to salvation because of the testimony of those whom they desire to emulate.

Some years ago, a young man in our church was told by his doctors that he had only a short time to live. His response was not one of regret or bitterness but of joy at the prospect of soon being with his Savior. Because of his confident faith and contentment in the face of death, one person I know of, and perhaps more, came to a saving knowledge of Christ.

During the Finnish-Russian war, seven captured Russian soldiers were sentenced to death by the Finnish army. The evening before they were to be shot, one of the soldiers began singing "Safe in the Arms of Jesus." Asked why he was singing such a song, he answered tearfully that he had heard it sung by a group of Salvation Army "soldiers" just three weeks earlier. As a boy he had heard his mother talk and sing of Jesus many times, but would not accept her Savior. The previous night, as he lay contemplating his execution, he had a vision of his mother's face, which reminded him of the hymn he had recently heard. The words of the song and verses from the Bible that he had heard long ago came to his mind. He testified before his fellow prisoners and his captors that he had prayed for Christ to forgive his sins and cleanse his soul and make him ready to stand before God. All the men, prisoners and guards alike, were deeply moved, and most spent the night praying, weeping, talking about spiritual things, and singing hymns. In the morning, just before the seven were shot, they asked to be able to sing once more "Safe in the Arms of Jesus," which they were allowed to do.

At least one other of the Russian soldiers had confessed Christ during the night. In addition, the Finnish officer in charge said, "What happened in the hearts of the others I don't know, but ... I was a new man from that hour. I had met Christ in one of His loveliest and youngest disciples, and I had seen enough to realize that I too could be His."

It may be that the first seeds of faith were planted in Paul's own heart by the testimony of Stephen, whose death the young Paul (then Saul) witnessed and whose confident and loving dying testimony he heard (Acts 7:59–8:1).

In 1 Corinthians 15:29 Paul may be affirming the truth that Christians who face death with joy and hope are a powerful testimony. The prospect of eternal life, of resurrection life, of reunion with loved ones, is a strong motive for people to listen to and accept the gospel. Resurrection is one of the greatest assurances that God gives to those who trust in His Son. For those who believe in Jesus Christ, the grave is not the end. At death our spirits are not absorbed back into some cosmic divine mind. When we die we will go immediately to be with the Lord—as an individual, personal being. Not only that, but one day our glorified bodies will rejoin our spirits, and we will live as whole, completed human beings throughout all of eternity with all who have loved and worshiped God.

Another way in which the believing **dead** are used as a means of salvation is through the hope of reunion. Many believers have been drawn to the Savior because of a strong desire to be united with a loved one who has gone to be with the Lord. I have never led a funeral service in which I did not make such an appeal. I have seen a husband who would not come to Christ until his wife died. Because he could not bear the thought of not seeing her again, committing his own life and eternity into the hands of the One he knew was her Lord was made more attractive. I have seen children come to Christ after their mother's death, motivated in part by the desire one day to be united with her. What her pleading and praying could not do, her death accomplished.

It is also true, of course, that the resurrection holds out great reunion hope for those who already are believers. The hope that sustained David after the death of his infant son was that, though "he will not return to me," "I shall go to him" (2 Sam 12:23). David knew that one day he and his son would be reunited.

Perhaps confused by some of the same pagan philosophy that plagued the Corinthian church, the Thessalonian believers were concerned because they thought their believing loved ones and friends who had died somehow had no prospect of a future life. "But we do not want you to be uninformed, brethren, about those who are asleep," Paul wrote them, "that you may not grieve, as do the rest who have no hope. For if we believe that Jesus died and rose again, even so God will bring with Him those who have fallen asleep in Jesus" (1 Thess 4:13–14). "Like you," he was assuring them, "they will be resurrected, and you will all be reunited by the Lord when He returns."

If there is no resurrection, no hope of a future life, Paul asked, why are people coming to Christ because of the testimony of believers who have died? **If the dead are not raised at all, why then are they** [many present Christians] **baptized for** [become believers because of the testimony of] **them** [deceased faithful believers]?

AN INCENTIVE FOR SERVICE

Why are we also in danger every hour? I protest, brethren, by the boasting in you, which I have in Christ Jesus our Lord, I die daily. If from human motives I fought with wild beasts at Ephesus, what does it profit me? If the dead are not raised, Let us eat and drink, for tomorrow we die. (15:30–32)

The second incentive that hope of the resurrection gives is that for service. Why, otherwise, would believers endure and sacrifice so much? If this life were the end, what would be the reason for Paul's and the other apostles' being **in danger every hour?**

If there were no resurrection of the believing dead, then suffering and dying for the sake of the gospel would be masochistic, suffering for suffering's sake. As Paul had already pointed out, "If we have hoped in Christ in this life only, we are of all men most to be pitied" (15:19).

The only thing that makes Christians willing to work hard, willing to suffer, willing to be abused and ridiculed, willing to endure in the work of Christ is that Christ's own supreme finished work, the redemption of sinners, will last past this present life (cf. Rom 8:18). What would be the purpose of suffering for Christ if we would never see Him face to face? What would be the purpose of winning others to Christ if they would never see Him face to face? Where would be the good news in such a gospel? Where would be the incentive for preaching or believing such a gospel?

Why make this life miserable if this life is all there is? Why be **in danger every hour,** if we have no security to look forward to? Why **die daily,** that is, risk your life in self-denying ministry, if death ends it all? **I protest,** Paul says vehemently, "You who deny the resurrection make a shambles of Christian service. Nothing makes sense if there is no resurrection." If Christ's resurrection on Easter morning was the only resurrection, as some of the Corinthians believed, then His being raised was no victory for us. He would not have conquered death but only made death a greater mockery for those who put their trust in Him.

If from human motives I fought with wild beasts at Ephesus, what does it profit me? What **human motives** could Paul have had for continually risking his safety and his life? We cannot be certain that Paul **fought** literal **wild beasts at Ephesus,** but it seems entirely possible that such was the case, and this interpretation is supported by tradition. It may be that Paul was speaking metaphorically of the wild crowd of Ephesians that was incited against him by the silversmith Demetrius (Acts 19:23–34). In any case, he was speaking of one of his many dangerous, life-threatening experiences.

Why would he have endured that, he was saying, and have continued to endure such things, if his only purpose and only hope was merely human and temporary? If we live only to die and remain dead, it makes more sense to say, **"Let us eat and drink, for tomorrow we die"**—a direct quotation from Isaiah 22:13 that reflected the hopeless and hedonistic view of the backslidden Israelites. It also reflects the dismal futility repeatedly expressed in Ecclesiastes: "'Vanity of vanities! All is vanity.' What advantage does man have in all his work which he does under the sun?" (Eccl 1:2–3).

The Greek historian Herodotus tells of an interesting custom of the Egyptians. "In social meetings among the rich, when the banquet was ended, a servant would often carry around among the guests a coffin, in which was a wooden image of a corpse carved and painted to resemble a dead person as nearly as possible. The servant would show it to each of the guests and would say, 'Gaze here and drink and be merry, for when you die such you shall be.'"

If this life is all there is, why should the sensual not rule? Why not grab all we can, do all we can, live it up all we can? If we die only to remain dead, hedonism makes perfect sense.

What would *not* make sense is the godly self-sacrifice of those "who by faith conquered kingdoms, performed acts of righteousness, obtained promises, shut the mouths of lions, quenched the power of fire, escaped the edge of the sword, ... wandering in deserts and mountains and caves and holes in the ground" (Heb 11:33–34, 38). Their hope that "they might obtain a better resurrection" (v. 35) would have been futile and empty.

"Jesus, the author and perfecter of faith, ... for the joy set before Him endured the cross, despising the shame, and has sat down at the right hand of the throne of God" (Heb 12:2). It was anticipation of the resurrection, of being raised to be again with His Father, that gave our Lord the motive for dying on our behalf. He was willing to die for us because He knew He would be raised for us.

AN INCENTIVE FOR SANCTIFICATION

Do not be deceived: "Bad company corrupts good morals." Become soberminded as you ought, and stop sinning; for some have no knowledge of God. I speak this to your shame. (15:33–34)

The third incentive the hope of resurrection gives is for sanctification. Looking forward to resurrection should lead to more godly living and spiritual maturity.

Verses 32 and 33 are closely related. Denying the resurrection destroys the incentives both for service and for sanctification. Why then bother serving the Lord or serving others in His name, and why bother to be holy and pure?

Paul warned the Corinthians that they should **not be deceived** about the danger of **bad company.** *Homilia* (**company**) basically means an association of people, but also can have the connotation of a lecture or sermon. It seems possible, therefore, that the Corinthians were both listening to some wrong teaching and associating with some evil people. Whether the teaching was in formal messages or not, it was **bad** and corrupting.

People who think wrongly invariably behave wrongly. Wrong behavior comes from wrong thinking, from wrong beliefs and wrong standards. It is impossible to associate regularly with wicked people without being contaminated both by their ideas and by their habits. The context implies that the **bad company** was teaching the heretical theology that there is no resurrection of the dead, and that bad theology had corrupted **good morals.**

Just as hoping in the resurrection is an incentive to obedience and holiness, so disbelief of it is an incentive to disobedience and immorality. As Paul has just pointed out, if there is no resurrection, we might as well **eat and drink, for tomorrow we die.** If death is the end, what great difference does it make what we do?

Some in the Corinthian congregation had **no knowledge of God,** and therefore no knowledge of His truth. Their bad theology was leading to bad behavior, especially because they denied the resurrection.

The Greek historian Thucydides reported that when a deadly plague came to Athens, "People committed every shameful crime and eagerly snatched at every lustful pleasure." They believed life was short and there was no resurrection, so they would have to pay no price for their vice. The Roman poet Horace wrote, "Tell them to bring wine and perfume and the too short-lived blossoms of the lovely rose while circumstance and age and the black threads of the three sisters fate still allow us to do so." Another Roman poet, Catullus, penned the lines: "Let's live my Lesbia and let's love, and let's value the tales of austere old men at a single half penny. Suns can set and then return again, but for us when once our brief light sets there is but one perpetual night through which we must sleep."

Without the prospect of a resurrection, and of the accountability it brings, there is no incentive for doing anything but what we feel like doing here and now. If behavior has no reward or condemnation, it is uncontrollable.

Become sober-minded as you ought, and stop sinning, Paul pleads in the imperative. "Those of you who believe in the resurrection know better, and you should be leading those who do not believe in the resurrection into a true **knowledge of God,** rather than allowing their heresy and their immorality to mislead and corrupt you." The apostle spoke **this to** [their] **shame.** They had the truth, but they did not fully believe it and therefore did not fully follow it. He commands them to cease the sin they were involved in.

What tremendous power the resurrection has, and what wonderful hope it gives! Jesus rose from the dead; He is alive; and we also shall live because one day He will raise us up to be with Him eternally. What greater incentive, what greater motive, could we have for coming to Him, for serving Him, and for living for Him?

05

OUR RESURRECTION BODIES

1 CORINTHIANS 15:35-49

B ut someone will say, "How are the dead raised? And with what kind of body do they come?" You fool! That which you sow does not come to life unless it dies; and that which you sow, you do not sow the body which is to be, but a bare grain, perhaps of wheat or of something else. But God gives it a body just as He wished, and to each of the seeds a body of its own. All flesh is not the same flesh, but there is one flesh of men, and another flesh of beasts, and another flesh of birds, and another of fish. There are also heavenly bodies and earthly bodies, but the glory of the heavenly is one, and the glory of the earthly is another. There is one glory of the sun, and another glory of the moon, and another glory of the stars; for star differs from star in glory. So also is the resurrection of the dead. It is sown a perishable body, it is raised an imperishable body; it is sown in dishonor, it is raised in glory; it is sown in weakness, it is raised in power; it is sown a natural body, it is raised a spiritual body. If there is a natural body, there is also a spiritual body. So also it is written, "The first man, Adam, became a living soul." The last Adam became a life-giving spirit. However, the spiritual is not first, but the natural; then the spiritual. The first man is from the earth, earthy; the second man is from heaven. As is the earthy, so also are those who are earthy; and as is the heavenly, so also are those who are

heavenly. And just as we have borne the image of the earthy, we shall also bear the image of the heavenly. (15:35–49)

The first major problem Paul deals with in chapter 15 is denial of general resurrection. Some of the Corinthians, though they had accepted the truth of Christ's resurrection, refused to believe that other men would or could be resurrected. Verses 12–34 show the error and dangers of such denial. Now the apostle deals with another troublesome issue, one that is really a part of the first, namely, the question of how a general resurrection could be possible. The idea of resurrecting all the human race seems inconceivable because of its complexity and the power demanded to accomplish it.

But someone will say, "How are the dead raised? And with what kind of body do they come?" (15:35)

Those in Corinth who denied the resurrection did so primarily because of the influence of gnostic philosophy, which considered the body to be inherently evil and only the spirit to be good. They therefore believed that resurrection of the body is *undesirable*. Paul now challenges the idea that resurrection also is *impossible*. "Supposing," they argued, "that resurrection were a good thing, how could it happen?"

Part of the problem some Greeks had may have been traceable to a false view of resurrection taught by many rabbis of that time. By misinterpreting such passages as Job 19:26 ("Yet from my flesh I shall see God"), they concluded that resurrection bodies will be identical to earthly bodies in every way. The writer of the Jewish apocryphal book of Baruch wrote, for example, that "the earth shall then [at the resurrection] assuredly restore the dead; it shall make no change in form, but as it has received so shall it restore." To Gnostics, that view made resurrection seem even *less* desirable and possible.

But why would anyone who acknowledges a creator God think His restoring bodies, in whatever way, would be any more difficult for Him than making them in the first place? As Paul asked before King Agrippa, "Why is it considered incredible among you people if God does raise the dead?" (Acts 26:8). Why do people still today, including some Christians, become perplexed and bothered about how God could restore the bodies of those who have been lost at sea, blown up in an explosion, or cremated? Why is His restoring those bodies more miraculous and unbelievable than His creating the universe? And besides, every dead body, no matter how well embalmed, eventually disintegrates.

Yet one objection to the idea of resurrection was, and still is, its seeming impossibility. **But someone will say,**

Paul's experience led him to anticipate, **"How are the dead raised?"** How could God possibly reassemble the bodies of everyone who has died throughout the ages of history? A closely related question was, **"And with what kind of body do they come?"**

In verses 36–49 Paul answers the questions of verse 35 in four ways: (1) he gives an illustration from nature, (2) he tells what kind of body resurrection bodies will be, (3) he contrasts earthly and resurrection bodies, and (4) he reminds them of the prototype resurrection, in which they already believed.

AN ILLUSTRATION OF RESURRECTION

You fool! That which you sow does not come to life unless it dies; and that which you sow, you do not sow the body which is to be, but a bare grain, perhaps of wheat or of something else. But God gives it a body just as He wished, and to each of the seeds a body of its own. (15:36–38)

Like denial of resurrection because it seems undesirable, denial of resurrection because it seems impossible came from the skepticism of pagan philosophy. It did not come from honest doubt or ignorance, and Paul responds accordingly: **You fool.** The word was used derisively of one who does not use or does not have understanding.

The questions mentioned in verse 35 were not those of someone who wanted to know but were the mocking taunts of someone who thought he already knew. As with most of the questions put to Jesus by the scribes, Pharisees, and Sadducees, the purpose was to entrap and embarrass, not discover truth.

To point up the foolishness of the objection, Paul gives a common illustration from nature. In three significant ways, resurrection is similar to the planting and growth of crops: the original form is dissolved, the original and final forms are different in kind, and yet the two forms have a continuity. Resurrection is not impossible, because it occurs on a small scale continuously in the plant world.

DISSOLUTION

First is the similarity of dissolution, or dying. **That which you sow does not come to life unless it dies.** When a seed is planted in the ground it dies, actually decomposing as a seed: it must cease to exist in its original form as a seed before it can **come to life** in its final form as a plant.

Applying the same figure, Jesus said, "Truly, truly, I say to you, unless a grain of wheat falls into the earth and dies, it remains by itself alone; but if it dies, it bears much fruit" (John 12:24). Before Christ could bear the fruit of salvation for us, He had to die. Likewise, before we can participate in the fruit of His resurrection, or bear fruit in His service, we too must die. "He who loves his life loses it; and he who hates his life in this world shall keep it to life eternal" (v. 25).

When Jesus was crucified, His earthly body died; it ceased to exist as an earthly body. Just as with growing crops, there had to be an end to the old before there could be a beginning of the new. In the case of men, one body will die to give life to another.

DIFFERENCE

Second, both in the growing of crops and in the resurrection of bodies there is a difference between the original and final forms. The seed loses its identity as a seed and becomes more and more like the mature plant. But the seed itself, **that which you sow**—whether it is **wheat or ... something else**—looks nothing like the mature plant, **the body which is to be.** Only after ceasing to be a seed does it become the mature plant the farmer harvests.

When Jesus was raised from the dead, His glorified body was radically different from the one which died. What came out of the grave was different from what was placed in the grave. It was no longer limited by time, space, and material substance. During His appearances, Jesus went from one place to another without traveling in any physical way. He appeared and disappeared at will, and entered rooms without opening the door (Luke 24:15, 31, 36; John 20:19; etc.). In His earthly body He had done none of those things. Resurrection changed Jesus' body in marvelous and radical ways, and at His return all resurrection bodies will be changed marvelously and radically.

CONTINUITY

Third, in spite of the differences, there is nevertheless a continuity between the old and the new. **But God gives it a body just as He wished, and to each of the seeds a body of its own.** The seed changes radically, but it continues as the same life form. A wheat seed does not become barley, and a flax seed does not become corn. **God** has given each type of seed **a body of its own,** whose identity continues into the grown plant.

After Jesus was raised, no one recognized Him unless He revealed Himself to them. But once revealed, He was recognizable. The disciples knew His face, and they recognized His wounded side and His pierced hands. In a similar way, our resurrected bodies as believers will have a continuity with the bodies we have now. Our bodies will die and they will change form, but they will still be our bodies. Surely it is not too hard to believe that the God who has worked this process daily through the centuries in His creation of plants can do it with men.

THE FORM OF RESURRECTION BODIES

All flesh is not the same flesh, but there is one flesh of men, and another flesh of beasts, and another flesh of birds, and another of fish. There are also heavenly bodies and earthly bodies, but the glory of the heavenly is one, and the glory of the earthly is another. There is one glory of the sun, and another glory of the moon, and another glory of the stars; for star differs from star in glory. So also is the resurrection of the dead. (15:39–42*a*)

These verses expand on Paul's previous point that our resurrection bodies will be different from our earthly bodies. Seeing the vast differences in God's creation, we should not question His ability to create bodies that are different and yet continuous.

All flesh is not the same flesh indicates the amazing variety of earthly bodies God has made. We need only look around us to see the virtually infinite assortment of created beings and things. In the biological world the flesh of men is absolutely distinct from the **flesh of beasts,** the **flesh of birds,** and the **flesh of fish.** All flesh is not of the same kind.

I have read that there are some six hundred octodecillion different combinations of amino acids. An octodecillion is 10 to the 108th power, or 1 followed by 108 zeros. Amino acids are the building blocks of all life.

Not only does each type of plant and animal life have a distinct pattern of amino acids, but each individual plant, animal, and human being has its own unique grouping of them. No two flowers, snowflakes, seeds, blades of grass, or human beings—even identical twins—are exactly alike. Yet each is completely identified with its own species or kind.

Those two facts make one of the strongest scientific evidences against evolution. No matter what we may eat, no matter how specialized or unbalanced our diet may be, and no matter what our environment may be, we will never change into another form of life. We may become healthier or more sickly, heavier or lighter, but we will never be anything but a human being and never any human being but the one we are. The biological codes are binding and unique. There is no repeatable or demonstrable scientific proof that one form of life has changed or could change into another.

There are also heavenly bodies, which obviously differ greatly from **earthly bodies** in **glory,** that is, in nature, manifestation, and form. Not only are the heavenly bodies vastly different from the earthly; they are greatly different from each other. The **sun** is greatly different from the **moon,** and both are different from the **stars.** From astronomy we know that many of what normally are called stars actually are planets, and therefore similar to the earth and moon, and that true stars are themselves suns. But Paul was speaking from the perspective of normal human observation, not from the perspective of science. From either perspective, however, his basic point is true. The stars generate their own light, while the planets and moons only reflect light produced by the stars. In that way the two types of heavenly bodies are greatly different in **glory,** that is, in character and manifestation.

Even **star differs from star in glory.** Donald Peattie has written,

> Like flowers, the stars have their own colors. At your first upward glance all gleam white as frost crystals, but single out this one and that for observation and you will find a subtle spectrum in the stars. The quality of their lights is determined by their temperatures. In the December sky you will see Aldebaran as pale rose, Rigel as bluish white and Betelgeuse orange to topaz yellow.

Every star is different, just as every plant is different, every animal is different, and every human being is different. God has infinite creative capacity, including the capacity to make infinite variety. Why would anyone think it hard for Him to re-create and resurrect human bodies, no matter what the form might be?

So also is the resurrection of the dead. Resurrection bodies will differ from earthly bodies just as radically as heavenly bodies differ from earthly. And resurrection bodies will be as individual and unique as are all the other forms of God's creation.

When Moses and Elijah appeared on the Mount of Transfiguration, they were as distinctly individual as they had been while living on earth. They did not then have resurrected bodies, but they were distinct beings of heaven, who one day will have distinct heavenly bodies. God is, not was, the God of Abraham, Isaac, and Jacob—the God of the living, not of the dead (Matt 22:32). Those patriarchs are not merely alive in heaven, but are alive as the same persons they were on earth. Jesus knows all His sheep by name (John 10:3), whether they are in heaven or still on earth. Our resurrection bodies will be as uniquely ours as our spirits and our names.

THE CONTRASTS OF RESURRECTION

It is sown a perishable body, it is raised an imperishable body; it is sown in dishonor, it is raised in glory; it is sown in weakness, it is raised in power; it is sown a natural body, it is raised a spiritual body. If there is a natural body, there is also a spiritual body. (15:42b–44)

Focusing more directly on the resurrection body, Paul here mentions specific ways, given as four sets of contrasts, in which our glorified bodies will be different from our earthly bodies.

PERISHABLE/IMPERISHABLE

The first contrast pertains to durability. One of the most obvious characteristics of all natural life, including human life, is that it is **perishable,** subject to deterioration and eventual death. Even in the healthy infant the process of aging and deterioration has begun. "All go to the same place. All came from the dust and all return to the dust" (Eccl 3:20). "For He Himself knows our frame; He is mindful that we are but dust. As for man, his days are like grass; as a flower of the field, so he flourishes. When the wind has passed over it, it is no more; and its place acknowledges it no longer" (Ps 103:14–16).

Even the healthiest of people, as they get older, become weaker and more subject to disease and various physical problems. Death, of course, rapidly accelerates decay. Martha objected to Lazarus's tomb being opened, because "by this time there will be a stench, for he has been dead four days" (John 11:39). The purpose of embalming is to retard deterioration of the body as long as possible. But even the remarkable Egyptian mummification could not prevent deterioration, much less restore life.

One of the tragic consequences of the Fall was that men's bodies from that time on were irreversibly mortal, subject to death. Without exception, every human being is **sown,** that is, born with, **a perishable body.**

But the resurrection body of the believer will be **raised an imperishable body.** "Blessed be the God and

Father of our Lord Jesus Christ, who according to His great mercy has caused us to be born again to a living hope through the resurrection of Jesus Christ from the dead, to obtain an inheritance which is imperishable and undefiled and will not fade away, reserved in heaven for you" (1 Pet 1:3–4). Our new bodies will know no sickness, decay, deterioration, or death. "When this perishable will have put on the imperishable, and this mortal will have put on immortality, then will come about the saying that is written, 'Death is swallowed up in victory'" (1 Cor 15:54).

DISHONOR/GLORY

The second contrast has to do with value and potential. At the Fall, man's potential for pleasing and serving God was radically reduced. Not only his mind and spirit but also his body became of immeasurably less value in doing what God had designed it to do. The creature that was made perfect, and in the very image of his Creator, was made to manifest his Creator in all that he did. But through sin, that which was created to honor God became characterized instead by **dishonor.**

We dishonor God by our inability to take advantage fully of what He has given us in His creation. We dishonor God by misusing and abusing the bodies through which He desires us to honor and serve Him. Even the most faithful believer dies with his body in a state of dishonor, a state of imperfection and incompleteness.

But that imperfect and dishonored body one day will be **raised in glory.** Throughout eternity our new immortal bodies will also be honorable bodies, perfected for pleasing, praising, and enjoying the Creator who made them and the Redeemer who restored them.

WEAKNESS/POWER

The third contrast has to do with ability. Our present bodies are characterized by **weakness.** We are weak not only in physical strength and endurance but also in resistance to disease and harm. Despite the marvelous natural protective mechanisms of the human body, no one is immune from breaking a bone, cutting a leg, catching various infections, and eventually from dying. We can and should minimize unnecessary dangers and risks to our bodies, which for believers are temples of the Holy Spirit (1 Cor 6:19–20). But we cannot completely protect them from harm, much less from death. Our earthly "temples" are inescapably temporary and fragile.

But not so our new bodies, which will be **raised in power.** We are not told what that power will entail, but it will be immeasurable compared to what we now possess. We will no longer have to say that "the spirit is willing, but the flesh is weak" (Matt 26:41). Anything our heavenly spirits determine to do our heavenly bodies will be able to accomplish.

Martin Luther said, "As weak as it [the human body of believers] is now without all power and ability when it lies in the grave, just so strong will it eventually become when the time arrives, so that not a thing will be impossible for it if it has a mind for it, and it will be so light and agile that in an instant it can float here below on earth or above in heaven."

NATURAL/SPIRITUAL

The fourth area of contrasts has to do with the sphere, or realm, of existence. Our earthly body is strictly **natural.** That is the only realm in which it can live and function. The physical body is suited for and limited to the physical world. Even with the imperfections and limitations caused by the Fall, our present bodies are wonderfully made for life on earth, marvelously suited for earthly living. But that is the only realm and the only living for which they are suited.

The new body of the believer, however, will be **raised a spiritual body.** Our spirits now reside in earthly bodies, but one day they will reside in spiritual bodies. In every way we then will be spiritual beings. In both spirit and body we will be perfectly suited for heavenly living.

"The sons of this age marry and are given in marriage," Jesus said, "but those who are considered worthy to attain to that age and the resurrection from the dead, neither marry, nor are given in marriage; for neither can they die anymore, for they are like angels, and are sons of God, being sons of the resurrection" (Luke 20:34–36).

In the resurrection everything about us will be perfected for all eternity. We will not be the same as angels, but will be "like" them in that we too will be perfectly equipped and suited for heavenly, spiritual, supernatural, living.

THE PROTOTYPE OF RESURRECTION

So also it is written, "The first man, Adam, became a living soul." The last Adam became a life-giving spirit. However, the spiritual is not first, but the natural; then the spiritual. The first man is from the earth, earthy; the second man is from heaven. As is the earthy, so also are those who are earthy; and as is the heavenly, so also are those who are heavenly. And just as we have borne the image of the earthy, we shall also bear the image of the heavenly. (15:45–49)

The fourth way in which Paul answers the questions "How are the dead raised? And with what kind of body do they come?" (v. 35) is by showing the prototype of resurrection and by further explaining the differences between natural and spiritual bodies.

He begins with a quotation from Genesis 2:7, with the addition of the two words **first** and **Adam. So also it is written, "The first man, Adam, became a living soul."** Adam was created with a natural body.

It was not glorified, but it was perfect and "good" in every way (Gen 1:31).

Adam and Eve originally were in a probationary period. Had they proved faithful rather than disobedient, their bodies would have been glorified and immortalized by eating the fruit of the tree of life, which they then could have eaten (see Gen 2:9). Because they sinned, however, they were put out of the garden lest they eat of the tree of life and live forever in a state of sin (3:22).

The last Adam, however, **became a life-giving spirit. The last Adam** is Jesus Christ. "As through the one man's disobedience the many were made sinners, even so through the obedience of the One the many will be made righteous. And ... as sin reigned in death, even so grace might reign through righteousness to eternal life through Jesus Christ our Lord" (Rom 5:19, 21; cf. vv. 12, 15). Through Adam we have inherited our natural bodies; through Christ we will inherit spiritual bodies in the resurrection.

Adam's was the prototype of our natural bodies, whereas Christ's was the prototype of our spiritual bodies. All the descendants of Adam have natural bodies, and all the descendants of Christ will have spiritual bodies. Christ's resurrection, therefore, was the prototype of all subsequent resurrection.

In verse 46 Paul points out the obvious: **However, the spiritual is not first, but the natural; then the**

spiritual. Every human being, starting with Adam and including Christ, has begun human life in a natural, physical body. The body that was raised from the dead on Easter morning had been a natural body, the incarnate body in which Christ was born and in which He lived and died. In the resurrection it was a spiritual, eternal body.

Adam, **the first man,** from whom came the natural race, originated on the earth, in fact was created directly **from the earth** (Gen 2:7). In every way, he was **earthy.** But Christ, called **the second man** because He has produced a spiritual race, existed eternally before He became a man. He lived on earth in a natural body, but He came **from heaven.** Adam was tied to earth; Christ was tied to heaven.

Because of our natural descent from Adam, we are a part of **those who are earthy.** But because of our inheritance in Jesus Christ, we also have become a part of **those who are heavenly.** In Adam we are **earthy;** in Christ we have become **heavenly.** One day, our natural bodies from Adam will be changed into our heavenly bodies from Christ.

And just as we have borne the image of the earthy, we shall also bear the image of the heavenly. Just as we will exchange Adam's natural body for Christ's spiritual body, we will also exchange Adam's **image** for Christ's.

From Jesus' postresurrection appearances, we get some idea of the greatness, power, and wonder of what our own resurrection bodies will be like. Jesus appeared and disappeared at will, reappearing again at another place far distant. He could go through walls or closed doors, and yet also could eat, drink, sit, talk, and be seen by those whom He wanted to see Him. He was remarkably the same, yet even more remarkably different. After His ascension, the angel told the amazed disciples, "This Jesus, who has been taken up from you into heaven, will come in just the same way as you have watched Him go into heaven" (Acts 1:11). The body the disciples saw after Jesus' resurrection is the same body that will be seen when He returns again.

Just as with our Lord, our bodies, which are now perishable, dishonored, weak, and natural, will be raised into bodies that are imperishable, glorious, powerful, and spiritual. That which hindered our service and manifestation of God will now be the marvelous channel of fulfillment. We will have His own power in which to serve and praise Him, and His own glory by which to manifest and magnify Him. "Then the righteous will shine forth as the sun in the kingdom of their Father" (Matt 13:43). In heaven we will radiate like the sun, in the blazing and magnificent glory which the Lord will graciously share with those who are His. Christ will "transform the body of our humble state into conformity with the body of His glory, by the exertion of the power that He has even to subject all things to Himself" (Phil 3:21).

We cannot imagine exactly what that will be like. Even our present spiritual eyes cannot envision our future spiritual bodies. "Beloved, now we are children of God, and it has not appeared as yet what we shall be. We know that, when He appears, we shall be like Him, because we shall see Him just as He is" (1 John 3:2). We will not see our own resurrected bodies, or even have our own resurrected bodies, until we first see Christ's.

"So the graveyards of man become the seed plots of resurrection," Erich Sauer beautifully observes, "and the cemeteries of the people of God become through the heavenly dew the resurrection fields of the promised perfection."

The coming resurrection is the hope and motivation of the church and of all believers. Whatever happens to our present bodies—whether they are healthy or unhealthy, beautiful or plain, short-lived or long-lived, or whether they are indulged or tortured— they are not our permanent bodies, and we should not hold them too dearly. Our blessed hope and assurance is that these created, natural bodies one day will be recreated as spiritual bodies. Although we have only a glimpse of what those new bodies will be like, it should be enough to know that "we shall be like Him."

06

VICTORY OVER DEATH

1 CORINTHIANS 15:50-58

Now I say this, brethren, that flesh and blood cannot inherit the kingdom of God; nor does the perishable inherit the imperishable. Behold, I tell you a mystery; we shall not all sleep, but we shall all be changed, in a moment, in the twinkling of an eye, at the last trumpet; for the trumpet will sound, and the dead will be raised imperishable, and we shall be changed. For this perishable must put on the imperishable, and this mortal must put on immortality. But when this perishable will have put on the imperishable, and this mortal will have put on immortality, then will come about the saying that is written, "Death is swallowed up in victory. O death, where is your victory? O death, where is your sting?" The sting of death is sin, and the power of sin is the law; but thanks be to God, who gives us the victory through our Lord Jesus Christ.

Therefore, my beloved brethren, be steadfast, immovable, always abounding in the work of the Lord, knowing that your toil is not in vain in the Lord. (15:50–58)

Someone has written,

There is a preacher of the old school but he speaks as boldly as ever. He is not popular, though the world is his parish and he travels every part of the globe and speaks in every language.

He visits the poor, calls upon the rich, preaches to people of every religion and no religion, and the subject of his sermon is always the same. He is an eloquent preacher, often stirring feelings which no other preacher could, and bringing tears to eyes that never weep. His arguments none are able to refute, nor is there any heart that has remained unmoved by the force of his appeals. He shatters life with his message. Most people hate him; everyone fears him. His name? Death. Every tombstone is his pulpit, every newspaper prints his text, and someday every one of you will be his sermon.

Thomas Gray wrote, "The boast of heraldry, the pomp of power and all that beauty and all that wealth e'er gave await alike the inevitable hour. The paths of glory lead but to the grave." As far as human power, beauty, wealth, and glory are concerned, that truth applies to Christians as much as to any others. But the hope of the Christian is not in such things, which he knows will end at the grave. The hope of the Christian is expressed by the epitaph Benjamin Franklin wrote for himself, engraved on his tombstone in the cemetery of Christ's Church in Philadelphia: "The body of Franklin, printer, like the cover of an old book, its contents torn out and stripped of its lettering and gilding, lies here food for worms. But the work will not be lost, for it will appear once more in a new and more elegant edition, revised and corrected by the Author."

That is the hope of the Christian and the message of 1 Corinthians 15. To the skeptics of every age, as to the skeptics in Corinth, the Holy Spirit through Paul gives a rebuke for denying the resurrection of the body (15:12, 35) and proclaims, "But now Christ has been raised from the dead, the first fruits of those who are asleep. For since by a man came death, by a man also came the resurrection of the dead. For as in Adam all die, so also in Christ all shall be made alive" (vv. 20–22).

In this longest chapter of the letter, the apostle has given the evidence for Christ's resurrection (vv. 1–11), the implications of denying bodily resurrection (vv. 12–19), the plan (vv. 20–28) and incentives (vv. 29–34) of resurrection, and a description and explanation of our resurrection bodies (vv. 35–49). In concluding this passage, he proclaims the marvelous victory that resurrection will bring for those who are Christ's.

Paul's concluding "victory song" has been put to music in such masterpieces as Handel's *Messiah* and Brahms's *Requiem*, and in many ways it is more appropriate to be sung than preached. Praising God in anticipation of resurrection, the apostle proclaims the great transformation, the great triumph, and the great thanksgiving that the raising of God's saints will bring, and then gives a great exhortation for holy living until that day comes.

THE GREAT TRANSFORMATION

Now I say this, brethren, that flesh and blood cannot inherit the kingdom of God; nor does the perishable inherit the imperishable. Behold, I tell you a mystery; we shall not all sleep, but we shall all be changed, in a moment, in the twinkling of an eye, at the last trumpet; for the trumpet will sound, and the dead will be raised imperishable, and we shall be changed. For this perishable must put on the imperishable, and this mortal must put on immortality. (15:50–53)

Paul reminds his readers again that the resurrection body will not be **flesh and blood,** which, though wonderfully suited for earth, is not at all suited for heaven and therefore **cannot inherit the kingdom of God. The kingdom of God** is not used here either in its universal sense, referring to God's ruling the universe, or in its spiritual sense, referring to His ruling in the human heart, but in its consummate sense, embodying both and referring to the eternal state, to heaven. "Just as we have borne the image of the earthy, we shall also bear the image of the heavenly" (v. 49).

Even Christ's own earthly body was "flesh and blood" (Heb 2:14) and had to be transformed before He could return to the Father. The human body is renewed every seven years, but that does not prevent its aging, deterioration, and eventual death. The human body is **perishable.** It is not suited for and cannot **inherit the imperishable.** It must be made different in order to inherit heaven, and it will *be* made different. "It is sown a perishable body, it is raised an imperishable body; it is sown in dishonor, it is raised in glory; it is sown in weakness, it is raised in power; it is sown a natural body, it is raised a spiritual body" (1 Cor 15:42–44). Like the seed that is planted, it continues its identity, but in a radically and wonderfully different form.

But what about believers who are living when Christ returns? Anticipating that question, Paul continues, **Behold, I tell you a mystery; we shall not all sleep.** As pointed out several times before, in the New Testament **mystery** always refers to that which had before been hidden and unknown but which is now revealed. The apostle now reveals that Christians who are alive when the Lord returns will not have to die (**sleep**) in order for their bodies to be changed. Those "who are alive and remain shall be caught up together with them in the clouds to meet the Lord in the air, and thus we shall always be with the Lord" (1 Thess 4:17). As believers are resurrected or caught up they **shall all be changed.** Whether believers die or are raptured, their bodies will be changed from the perishable to the imperishable, from the natural to the spiritual. Since the perishable cannot inherit the imperishable, Enoch and Elijah must have been changed in the same way that raptured believers will be changed. In any case, **all** believers will be equally equipped for heaven (cf. Phil 3:20–21).

Both for the resurrected and for the raptured, the change will be **in a moment, in the twinkling of an eye.** It will not be a process, a supernatural metamorphosis. It will be an instantaneous recreation from one form to the other, from the earthy to the heavenly. **Moment** is from *atomos*, from which we get the word *atom*, and denotes that which cannot be cut, or divided, the smallest conceivable quantity. In the smallest possible amount of time, our perishable bodies will be made imperishable. To further emphasize and illustrate the speed of the change, Paul says that it will occur **in the twinkling of an eye.** *Rhipē* (**twinkling**) literally means to hurl, and was used to refer to any rapid movement. The **eye** can move much faster than any other visible part of our bodies, and Paul's point was that the change will be extremely fast, instantaneous.

This change will occur **at the last trumpet.** I do not think that this **trumpet** necessarily will be the **last** heavenly trumpet ever to be sounded. It will, however, be the last as far as living Christians are concerned, for it will **sound** the end of the church age, when all believers will be removed from the earth. "For the Lord Himself will descend from heaven with a shout, with the voice of the archangel, and with the trumpet of God; and the dead in Christ shall rise first. Then we who are alive and remain shall be caught up together with them in the clouds to meet the Lord in the air, and thus we shall always be with the Lord" (1 Thess 4:16–17). By that trumpet, God will summon all of His people to Himself (cf. Exod 19:16; Isa 27:13).

During the Civil War, a group of soldiers had to spend a winter night without tents in an open field. During the night it snowed several inches, and at dawn the chaplain reported a strange sight. The snow-covered soldiers looked like the mounds of new graves, and when the bugle sounded reveille, a man immediately rose from each mound of snow, dramatically reminding the chaplain of this passage from 1 Corinthians.

Speaking of the coming resurrection day, Jesus said, "I will come again, and receive you to Myself; that where I am, there you may be also" (John 14:3). As He ascended to heaven, the angels told the onlooking disciples, "This Jesus, who has been taken up from you into heaven, will come in just the same way as you have watched Him go into heaven" (Acts 1:11). With Paul, every believer should be "looking for the blessed hope and the appearing of the glory of our great God and Savior, Christ Jesus" (Titus 2:13).

Because earthly, natural bodies cannot occupy the eternal kingdom, such a day and such a moment has to be, **for this perishable** [that which is subject to decay] **must put on the imperishable, and this mortal must put on immortality.** The word translated **put**

on was commonly used of putting on clothing, and pictures our redeemed spirits being dressed with redeemed bodies (cf. 2 Cor 5:1–5).

THE GREAT TRIUMPH

But when this perishable will have put on the imperishable, and this mortal will have put on immortality, then will come about the saying that is written, "Death is swallowed up in victory. O death, where is your victory? O death, where is your sting?" The sting of death is sin, and the power of sin is the law. (15:54–56)

Christ's resurrection broke the power of death for those who believe in Him, and death is no longer master over them because "death no longer is master over Him" (Rom 6:9). But death is still the enemy of man. Even for Christians, it violates our dominion of God's creation, it breaks love relationships, it disrupts families, and causes great grief in the loss of those dear to us. We no longer need fear death, but it still invades and torments us while we are mortal.

But one day, when Christ returns, the **perishable** that "*must* put on the imperishable" (v. 53) **will have put on the imperishable,** and the mortal that "must put on immortality" **will have put on immortality.** Then will come the great triumph that Isaiah predicted, when **death is swallowed up in victory.** The Isaiah text reads, "He [the Lord of Hosts] will swallow up death for all time" (Isa 25:8; cf. v. 6). When the great transformation comes, the great victory will come.

The well-known commentator R. C. H. Lenski writes,

> Death is not merely destroyed so that it cannot do further harm while all of the harm which it has wrought on God's children remains. The tornado is not merely checked so that no additional homes are wrecked while those that were wrecked still lie in ruin.... Death and all of its apparent victories are undone for God's children. What looks like a victory for death and like a defeat for us when our bodies die and decay shall be utterly reversed so that death dies in absolute defeat and our bodies live again in absolute victory (*The Interpretation of St. Paul's First and Second Epistles to the Corinthians* [Minneapolis: Augsburg, 1963], pp. 744–45).

Quoting another prophet (Hos 13:14), Paul taunts death: **O death, where is your victory? O death, where is your sting?** To continue with that metaphor, Paul implies that **death** left its **sting** in Christ, as a bee leaves its stinger in its victim. Christ bore the whole of death's sting in order that we would have to bear none of it.

To make his point, the apostle reminds his readers that **the sting of death is sin.** The harm in death is caused by sin; in fact, death itself is caused by sin.

"Therefore, just as through one man sin entered into the world, and death through sin, and so death spread to all men, because all sinned" (Rom 5:12). Only where there is sin can death deal a fatal blow. Where sin has been removed, death can only interrupt the earthly life and usher in the heavenly. That is what Christ has done for those who trust in Him. Our "sins are forgiven for His name's sake" (1 John 2:12). Death is not gone, but its sting, sin, is gone. "For if by the transgression of the one, death reigned through the one, much more those who receive the abundance of grace and of the gift of righteousness will reign in life through the One, Jesus Christ" (Rom 5:17).

It is not, of course, that Christians no longer sin, but that the sins we commit are already covered by Christ's atoning death, so that sin's effect is not permanently fatal. "The blood of Jesus His Son cleanses us from all sin" (1 John 1:7). But for those who do not believe, death's vsting tragically remains forever.

Paul continues to explain the sequence leading to death by mentioning that **the power of sin is the law.** God's law reveals God's standards, and when they are broken they reveal man's sin. If there were no law, obviously there could be no transgression. "Where there is no law neither is there violation" (Rom 4:15). But men die because they break that law.

What about those who do not know God's law, who have never even heard of, much less read, His Word?

Paul tells us in Romans that when "Gentiles who do not have the Law do instinctively the things of the Law, these, not having the Law, are a law to themselves, in that they show the work of the Law written in their hearts, their conscience bearing witness, and their thoughts alternately accusing or else defending them" (2:14–15). Anyone, therefore, who goes against his conscience goes against God's law just as surely as anyone who knowingly breaks one of the Ten Commandments. That is the reason men are doomed to die (Rom 3:23; 6:23).

THE GREAT THANKSGIVING

But thanks be to God, who gives us the victory through our Lord Jesus Christ. (15:57)

Because of Jesus' perfect obedience to the law (Rom 5:19) and the satisfaction He made for its victims, those who trust in Him "are not under law, but under grace," having "been released from the Law" (Rom 6:14; 7:6). Jesus has both fulfilled the law and fulfilled righteousness. Because His life was sinless and therefore fulfilled the law, His death conquered sin.

Paul gives thanks to the One who will give us the great transformation of our bodies and who has made the great triumph over sin and death. That which we could never do for ourselves **God** has done for us **through our Lord Jesus Christ.** We cannot live sinlessly and thereby fulfill the law, nor can we remove sin once we have committed it, or remove its consequence, which is death. But on our behalf, Jesus Christ lived a sinless life, fulfilling the law; removed our sin by Himself paying the penalty for it, satisfying God with a perfect sacrifice; and conquered death by being raised from the dead. All of that great **victory** He accomplished for us and **gives** to **us.** "Christ redeemed us from the curse of the Law, having become a curse for us" (Gal 3:13). He took our curse and our condemnation and gives us victory in their place.

How can we do anything but thank and praise God for what He has done for us? He has promised us an imperishable, glorious, powerful, and spiritual body for one that is perishable, dishonorable, weak, and natural. He promises us the heavenly in exchange for the earthly, the immortal in exchange for the mortal. We know these promises are assured because He has already given us victory over sin and death.

For Christians, death has no more power (Heb 2:14–15), because God has taken away our sin. For Christians, death is but the passing of our spirits from this life to the next, the leaving of earth and going to be with Christ. Paul had only one reason for wanting to remain on earth: to continue his ministry for Christ on behalf of others. But for his own benefit and joy he had but one desire: "to depart and be with Christ, for that is very much better" (Phil 1:23–24).

In Christ's victory over death, death's sting is removed; it is declawed, defanged, disarmed, destroyed. "And death and Hades were thrown into the lake of fire, ... and He shall wipe away every tear from their eyes; and there shall no longer be any death; there shall no longer be any mourning, or crying, or pain" (Rev 20:14; 21:4).

THE GREAT EXHORTATION

Therefore, my beloved brethren, be steadfast, immovable, always abounding in the work of the Lord, knowing that your toil is not in vain in the Lord. (15:58)

If we really believe and if we are truly thankful that our resurrection is sure, that we will be transformed from the perishable, dishonorable, weak, natural, mortal, and earthy to the imperishable, glorious, powerful, spiritual, immortal, and heavenly—we should **therefore** prove our assurance and our thankfulness by being **steadfast, immovable** [negative] and **always abounding** [positive] **in the work of the Lord.**

Hedraios (**steadfast**) literally refers to being seated, and therefore to being settled and firmly situated. *Ametakinetōs* (**immovable**) carries the same basic idea but with more intensity. It denotes being totally immobile and motionless. Obviously, Paul is talking about our being moved *away from* God's will, not to our being moved *within* it. Within His will, we are to be **always abounding in the work of the Lord.** But we should not move a hairbreadth away from His will, continually being careful not to be "tossed here and there by waves, and carried about by every wind of doctrine, by the trickery of men, by craftiness in deceitful scheming" (Eph 4:14).

Gordon Clark gives a helpful paraphrase of this verse: "Therefore we should mortify emotion, be steadfast, unchangeable, not erratic and scatterbrained, easily discouraged, and should multiply our good works in the knowledge that the Lord will make them profitable."

If our confident hope in the resurrection wavers, we are sure to abandon ourselves to the ways and standards of the world. If there are no eternal ramifications or consequences of what we do in this life, the motivation for selfless service and holy living is gone.

On the other hand, when our hope in the resurrection is clear and certain we will have great motivation to be **abounding in the work of the Lord.** *Perisseuō* (**abounding**) carries the idea of exceeding the requirements, of overflowing or overdoing. In Ephesians 1:7–8 the word is used of God's *lavishing* on us "the riches of His grace." Because God has so abundantly overdone Himself for us who deserve nothing from Him, we should determine to overdo ourselves (if that were possible) in service to Him, to whom we owe everything.

What a word Paul gives to the countless Christians who work and pray and give and suffer as little as they can! How can we be satisfied with the trivial, insignificant, short-lived things of the world? How can we "take it easy" when so many around us are dead spiritually and so many fellow believers are in need of edification, encouragement, and help of every sort? When can a Christian say, "I've served my time, I've done my part; let others do the work now"?

Reasonable rest is important and necessary. But if we err, Paul is saying, it should be on the side of doing more work for the Lord, not less. Leisure and relaxation are two great modern idols, to which many Christians seem quite willing to bow down. In proper proportion recreation and diversions can help restore our energy and increase our effectiveness. But they also can easily become ends in themselves, demanding more and more of our attention, concern, time, and energy. More than one believer has relaxed and hobbied himself completely out of the **work of the Lord.**

Some of God's most faithful and fruitful saints have lived to old age and been active and productive in His service to the end. Many others, however, have seen their lives shortened for the very reason that they were **abounding,** overflowing and untiring, in service to Christ. Henry Martyn, the British missionary to India and Persia, determined "to burn out for God," which he did before he was thirty-five. David Brainerd, one of the earliest missionaries to American Indians, died before he was thirty. We know very little of Epaphroditus, except that he was a "brother and fellow worker and fellow soldier" of Paul's who "came close to death for the work of Christ, risking his life" (Phil 2:25, 30). He became so lost in godly service that he literally became sick unto death because of it.

Until the Lord returns, there are souls to reach and ministries of every sort to be accomplished. Every Christian should work uncompromisingly as the Lord has gifted and leads. Our money, time, energy, talents, gifts, bodies, minds, and spirits should be invested in nothing that does not in some way contribute to **the work of the Lord.** Our praise and thanksgiving must be given hands and feet. James tells us, "For just as the body without the spirit is dead, so also faith without works is dead" (Jas 2:26).

Our work for the Lord, if it is truly for Him and done in His power, cannot fail to accomplish what He wants accomplished. Every good work believers do in this life has eternal benefits that the Lord Himself guarantees. "Behold, I am coming quickly," Jesus says, "and My reward is with Me, to render to every man according to what he has done" (Rev 22:12). We have God's own promise that our **toil** [labor to the point of exhaustion] **is not in vain in the Lord.**

BIBLIOGRAPHY

Barclay, William. *The Letters to the Corinthians.* Philadelphia: Westminster, 1956.

Clark, Gordon H. *First Corinthians.* Nutley, NJ: Presbyterian and Reformed, 1975.

Godet, F. L. *The First Epistle to the Corinthians.* Grand Rapids: Zondervan, 1971.

Grosheide, F. W. *The First Epistle to the Corinthians.* The New International Commentary on the New Testament. Grand Rapids: Eerdmans, 1953.

Hodge, Charles. *An Exposition of the First Epistle to the Corinthians.* Grand Rapids: Eerdmans, 1974.

Lenski, R. C. H. *The Interpretation of St. Paul's First and Second Epistles to the Corinthians.* Minneapolis: Augsburg, 1963.

Morgan, G. Campbell. *The Corinthian Letters of Paul.* Old Tappan, NJ: Revell, 1946.

Morris, Leon. *The First Epistle of Paul to the Corinthians.* The Tyndale New Testament Commentaries. London: The Tyndale Press, 1958.

Robertson, A. T., and Plummer, Alfred. *A Critical and Exegetical Commentary on the First Epistle of St. Paul to the Corinthians.* Edinburgh: T. & T. Clark, 1914.

INDEXES

INDEX OF SCRIPTURE

INDEX OF SUBJECTS

the MACARTHUR
NEW TESTAMENT
COMMENTARY

THE MACARTHUR NEW TESTAMENT COMMENTARY series is a verse-by-verse exposition of the New Testament that brings the believer into fellowship with God. Written for pastor and layperson alike, every commentary examines the history, language, and theology of the text to provide an accurate interpretation of each passage. The goal is for the believer to understand and apply God's Word to daily life in order to be conformed to the image of the Lord Jesus Christ.

JOHN MACARTHUR PUBLISHING GROUP
LOS ANGELES, CALIFORNIA